Lost in the Hell Hole

*A TRUE STORY OF SURVIVAL
AGAINST ALL ODDS*

Order this book online at www.trafford.com
or email orders@trafford.com

Most Trafford titles are also available at major online book retailers.

Printed in Victoria, BC, Canada.

ISBN: 978-1-4269-1974-9 (sc)

*Our mission is to efficiently provide the world's finest, most comprehensive
book publishing service, enabling every author to experience success.
To find out how to publish your book, your way, and have it available
worldwide, visit us online at www.trafford.com*

Trafford rev. 8/3/2010

 **www.trafford.com**

North America & international
toll-free: 1 888 232 4444 (USA & Canada)
phone: 250 383 6864 ♦ fax: 812 355 4082

Lost in the Hell Hole

A TRUE STORY OF SURVIVAL
AGAINST ALL ODDS

LOST IN THE HELL HOLE

A True Story of Survival Against All Odds

By:

WILLIAM C. BUSH
AND
YVONNE ROSE BUSH

Bush Publishing
P.O. Box 12514
Prescott, AZ 86304

Cover by:
Kevn Lambson
Idear Studios
Kevnlamb@gmail.com

Interior design by:
Tara Fort
tara@versatility4u.com

Edited by:
Lee Howard
Aleehoward2002@yahoo.com

DEDICATION

*T*his book is dedicated to the memory of Joe, a boy who came to live with my family at a difficult time in his life. Joe died in the military at the age of nineteen. He was Chris's older brother. I felt that brothers should be together. Joe was a good boy and my family and I will always have caring memories of him.

ACKNOWLEDGEMENTS

I have been working on this book for the past few years. Putting this story down on paper has helped me take a good look at myself. There have been many situations since this adventure that have taught me to slow down a little before I jump in with both feet.

I cannot thank the entire rescue team enough. They willingly put their lives on the line for my boys and me. The helicopter pilots, paramedics and all of those who worked very long hours in unforgiving conditions will always have a special place in my heart.

A special thanks to my brother-in-law Arlo, and his wife for all their time and effort co-ordinating the search. They didn't give up on us. We would not have made it out alive without them.

My hunting partner, Chuck, made his way to the guard shack and got the search started. He is still a good friend.

Thank you to my wife, Yvonne, for helping me write this book. She has spent a lot of time putting this together. Special thanks to Kevn Lambson for creating the outstanding cover for this book. A sincere thank you to Lee Howard for editing, and Tara Fort for the interior design. Any errors in this book are my responsibility and not theirs.

Table of Contents

LOST IN THE HELL HOLE
BY WILLIAM C. BUSH
AND
YVONNE ROSE BUSH

CHAPTER ONE

THIS IS THE WAY IT WAS

In all your ways acknowledge Him and He will make your paths straight.

Proverbs 3:6

I grew up in western Pennsylvania, sixth in a family of twelve kids. By the time I come along, needless to say, my mom was a little worn out. She had five kids in about that many years. She had twelve kids by the time she reached the age of thirty-five. My mom worked very hard cleaning houses and cooking in restaurants as she could, but most of the time we were on welfare.

The Salvation Army helped us out a lot as well. There would have been many times we would have gone to bed hungry if it hadn't been for the kindness of the Salvation Army. We ate beans cooked about every way beans can be cooked. The food wasn't fancy, but it sure tasted good to me. Mom burned the food quite often, but we ate it anyway. We were all pretty hungry by mealtime.

My mom didn't smoke or drink and could make a few dollars go further than you could ever imagine. I never knew how she did it, but somehow she managed to feed us and pay the bills. Dad rarely helped her. He felt she had us and she was responsible for us. Fortunately she loved us and did her best. It was a very hard life for her.

Dad forbade Mom from ever going to church. Whenever he was home, we couldn't attend church. When he was gone, we all went to church. Mom took us to any church that was helping us out at the time. It was no small task feeding and clothing twelve kids. We went to the Seventh Day Adventist Church, Jehovah Witness Meetings, Christian Missionary Alliance, Methodist, Baptist, and any other church that gave us food and clothes. We all liked to sit right up at the front of the church. Like most kids, we didn't want to miss anything.

One day the pastor from the church we were attending knocked at our front door. Mom graciously invited him in and offered him a seat and a cup of coffee. We were very pleased that he took time out of his busy day to visit us. All of us were pretty excited to see the pastor. He seemed to be in a hurry, but he did sit down and talked with Mom for a while. We all sat down near him. A little later he said that he had a message for Mom from the people in the church.

The leaders in the church had sent him to tell Mom that if she wanted to continue bringing her children to the church, we all had to sit way in the back of the church because our clothes looked bad and we were dirty. He told her, "If you can get some better looking clothes and bathe your children, you can sit closer to the front." The people in the church were complaining to the pastor. They said we made the church look bad. We probably made it smell bad too!

Mom was very hurt and wept for quite awhile after

he left. I was young and didn't know what was really happening, but I didn't like seeing my mom cry. She tried to clean us up and make us presentable, but the pastor continued to complain to her about our appearance. He said that he was trying to build a church, and a woman with so many children and no husband in the home made his church look bad. Eventually, all of us except my older sister quit going to church.

My older brother Tom refused to attend any church for many years, as a result. Later in life Tom did go to church when he visited us, but he never appeared very comfortable. He was happy when the service was over and he could go home. My older sister married a Christian man and has been an active part of her church all her life. Over the years, my other brothers and sisters attended church occasionally. It has never been a priority in their lives.

I didn't see my dad very often because he only came home once in awhile, long enough to get my mother pregnant, and then he was gone again. We were always relieved when he left. He was a small man filled with an incredible amount of hate and anger. He had a mean streak as long as your arm. He would beat Mom and us kids for almost anything. He liked to make us all stand in a row. He would tell us all to bend over and touch our ankles, then he would just go down the row, beating us all with his belt. If he felt one kid did something wrong, he beat us all. It bothered me that he seemed to enjoy beating us. He beat the little girls as well as the boys. I was too young to protect the little girls.

Mom had Kate, my oldest sister, when she was barely fifteen years old. She had very little help taking care of us. Dad told all of us that it cost him ten thousand dollars to raise each one of us. He insisted that we pay him back before he would allow us to leave home. As soon as I reached eighteen, I was gone. Dad was so angry with me that he did not allow me to come home for two years. He didn't allow me to see my mother during that time. I really missed my mother and was very happy when I got to see her again.

We lived in what now would be called the inner city or the ghetto. Call it whatever you want, it was the worst part of town. My brother and I wandered the streets and did pretty much whatever we wanted to do. We liked to play in the water most of all. We spent a lot of time playing down by the Allegheny River. There were homeless people living along the river, but they never bothered us much and we didn't bother them. In those days we called them bums.

We jumped off an old pump house into the river with an inner tube around us before we even knew how to swim. No one had to teach us. Out of necessity, we learned to swim real fast!

Our favorite place to search for things was at the city dump. Our house was just a couple blocks from the city dump. We would dig through all the garbage and find all kinds of "treasures." I found many things, among them six old spoons that I took to an antique store and sold for eleven dollars. I thought I was a millionaire!

One day I saw something sparkling under quite a bit of garbage. I couldn't see exactly what it was, so I kept digging and digging through the garbage. Finally I reached it and could see that it was a ring. It looked like it might be a diamond! I cleaned it up the best I could, then took it home and proudly gave it to my mother. She hugged me and thanked me and wore it all the rest of her life. She gave it to my daughter shortly before she passed away. Oh, by the way, it was one of the prettiest diamond rings you've ever seen!

The Salvation Army would give us all they could for the month. When they had given us as much as they could and we had no more food or money, they would give Mom a job cleaning houses. She always had to take some of us kids with her, so her jobs didn't last very long. I remember one Christmas in particular; Dad was gone and the Salvation Army gave us a lot of presents. I didn't know that getting Christmas presents was so much fun! That was our best Christmas and the only one that I remember.

Even though we lived in the worst part of town, we were fairly safe, mostly because of our sheer numbers. I had three older brothers and as a result, no one messed with me. My older brothers were pretty tough. Even though my life was difficult, my older brothers had it even worse. They suffered the full measure of my dad's wrath. We were all very strong, I guess from eating all those beans.

My two older brothers, Bud and Tom, had jobs setting pins at the local bowling alley. I tagged along with them, along with my brother Jim, who was just sixteen months older than I. The owner allowed us to sit and watch the bowlers as long as we behaved ourselves. One night some of the employees didn't show up for work and the owner asked my brother if he would like to set pins. He was ten years old at the time.

I asked the owner, "Why can't I set pins too?" He told me that I was too young. I was only nine years old. As the night got busier and busier, he come over to me and asked if I thought I could handle it. I said, "If my brothers can do it, I can do it." That night I started setting pins and kept the job for the next four years.

We would jump up on the back, waiting for people to throw the bowling balls. More often than not, we would get hit with pins that were flying. As soon as a person threw the second ball, I jumped down in the pit and put the ball in the return rack. Then I pushed the lever with my foot to pop the spikes up out of the floor. After that, we set the pins, each of which had a hole on the bottom. We dropped the spikes down and jumped out of the pit before the next ball came barreling toward us. That's when I usually got hit in the shins! That's also about the time I learned my first cuss words.

If we worked fast and people didn't fool around too much, we could make fifty cents an hour. We would set pins until midnight and then had to walk home afterward. When Dad was home, he would take whatever money we made. He reminded me often that it cost him ten thousand dollars to raise each of us and we had to pay him back before we could leave home.

I usually slept in school. I was tired from setting pins the night before. I put my head down on my desk and slept through most of the classes. Usually my teachers let me sleep, except Miss Maurine. She would smack my hands with her ruler until I woke up. It really hurt when she smacked my hands with the ruler. She was determined that I was going to learn something in her classroom. She had no mercy!

Later, I got a job delivering papers and made enough money to buy a bike. I learned to bury money on my way home from work and go back later when Dad was gone and get it. One of my brothers told Dad and I got in a lot of trouble. It was the worst beating and the last beating he ever gave me. He made me dig up the money and give it to him.

In my teens, I went to work for Altman's Feed Store in New Kensington. My job was to load bags of feed onto a truck and deliver them to farms. I also unloaded the bags at the farms. Doing this day in and day out made me very muscular and strong. The stronger I got, the more my dad seemed to be intimidated.

My dad often reminded me that he wasn't afraid of me. One day, my brother Jim, Dad, and I were riding in the truck. Dad was sitting in the middle and Jim was driving. For some strange reason he hit my arm very lightly and said, "See, I'm not afraid of you." It struck me funny at the time. It really made him mad when I laughed at him. We both knew that I was much stronger than he. He knew he could not control me with fear any longer. He never tried to hit me with his hand or a belt again.

My two oldest brothers saw a lot more hardship with my dad than I did. At a very young age, he made them get jobs and work very hard. At one time my oldest brother, Bud, held three jobs and had to bring every penny he earned home and give it to my dad. My older brother was very thin and did not look healthy. He worked continuously and rarely went to school. He died in his mid teens. He didn't get the opportunity to have friends or enjoy the usual things that most young people do. It seemed to me that he didn't have much of a chance in life.

My second oldest brother, Tom, also worked two and three jobs to support the family. Dad would take the money he and Bud earned to buy cigarettes and other things for himself. They had seen him beat Mom and the vulnerable younger kids so often that they decided that he was never going to harm any of them ever again. They felt that he had to be stopped.

He was so mean and full of rage and had done so much harm to the younger children. My two older brothers also felt that they were supporting the family. Dad rarely held a job. He would work off and on at jobs, but never kept any job very long. He was known around town to be a very good mechanic and even had an opportunity to become a partner in a garage. He didn't, and the man who wanted him as a partner became quite successful.

Bud and Tom decided they were going to kill him. They talked and talked about it and developed a plan over a long period of time. Finally the plan was perfect and they were all set. Everything was in place, and it would look like an accident. No one would ever suspect. When the day came, everything was ready. Their plan was falling into place even better than they planned. When it came time to do it, at the very last minute, they both decided not to. I'm glad they changed their minds. I'm sure they were too.

As it turned out, Dad died in his early fifties and Mom went on to live a good, long life. She bought her own home and furniture and enjoyed her children, grandchildren, and even great-grandchildren. God blessed her and honored her faithfulness. She gave her heart to the Lord after he died and attended church faithfully the remainder of her life.

She never remarried, even though she had opportunities. She said that she did not want to go through all of the heartbreak again. Dad had never allowed her to go to church and she could not have any friends. Her abuser kept her isolated from family and friends, typical of most perpetrators. After his death, she developed many lasting friendships and traveled internationally as well as all over the United States. She loved to visit her children and grandchildren.

Mom worked hard to keep us all together. Dad could have cared less. On one occasion he told my mom she looked tired and needed a rest. He offered to take her to a hotel in town. He said that he would take care of all of us and she didn't have to worry about us.

He had a plan and wanted Mom out of the house to get his plan in motion. While resting at the hotel, she got wind of his plan and headed straight home. He had called child welfare and told them his wife had left him and all of his kids. He told them that he needed homes for his kids. He was trying to put all of us in foster homes and orphanages. My mother was generally quite passive when it came to Dad, but let me tell you, when she got home she took care of him and his plan real quick! He left in a big hurry and stayed away a long time.

She worked at any job she could get and somehow managed to keep a roof over our heads and clothes on our backs. My dad provided very little, if any, financial support for us. Once in awhile he would give Mom a little bit of money. Usually he spent what money he earned on himself or on other people. He never stayed with any job very long.

Watch for a book coming out soon titled, *Alone in the Night; The Story of Bessie Ruth.* It will be the story of my mom's life. She felt her story would help other women who are in difficult circumstances and don't know what to do.

Somehow, through all of the hardships I faced as a child, I managed to keep some level of balance in my life. I give my mother the credit for that. Mom was always there and she always worked very hard. She also somehow maintained a pretty good sense of humor. It seems to me that if children have one good parent, they can make it. I had that one good parent.

I didn't know it at the time, but I was developing strength and survival skills that were going to take me through an ordeal of body and mind twenty years later. Little did I know that my Christian faith would be tested as never before.

As soon as I was old enough, I enlisted in the Army. Looking back, I think that I really grew up in the military. It was the first time that I had running water and an inside toilet. My years in the Army were the most relaxing time of my entire life. I didn't have to worry about where my next meal was coming from. I had a roof over my head, food, a place to sleep, and it was clean. I had led a pretty tough life, so the military discipline was not difficult for me.

While serving in the Army, I earned my GED, as well as learned to cook. My younger sister asked me for my recipe for chipped beef over toast. It was good food and I was more than willing to accommodate her. She called me a few days later and said, "This recipe is for three hundred men!" It took some doing to figure that one out!

I married Yvonne and we had three children, two boys and a girl. We moved to sunny Southern California. I was able to get a good job with a printing company that took care of us. Our life was picture perfect; if you know what I mean. We had three healthy children and a four-bedroom house in a nice development.

We were living the Southern California dream and loving every minute of it. We spent a lot of time at the ocean beaches. We enjoyed body surfing the waves at Huntington Beach. Our sons, Don and Steve, enjoyed playing in the ocean waves. Our daughter Billie Jean spent hours digging in the sand. The beaches were good places to go for a day of family fun. Yvonne and I enjoyed body surfing the waves, as well. What carefree summer days we spent at the beach!

We always wanted a house in the country with a few acres and a year- round creek flowing through it. I felt it would be fun for all of us and healthy for our children, rather than living in the big city. We went to Oregon to visit relatives, and we all fell in love with the tall pine trees, the good fishing and most of all the deer hunting.

I saw an ad in the *Oregonian* newspaper for printers wanted for a new plant opening up in Beaverton, Oregon. I went to talk with them and they hired me on the spot. They even paid for moving us from California to Beaverton. It doesn't get any better than that! The only catch was they wanted me in Oregon in three weeks!

I had a house to sell and a lot of packing to do real fast. We got it all done and were up in Oregon lickety-split. I bought us a five-acre place in some of the prettiest country you've ever seen. Our acreage had a year-round creek, tall, thick woods, and beautiful, green Oregon ferns. My boys and I built a house that was big and, well, when we were finished it looked like a country lodge.

My wife and I became Christians at Aloha Baptist Church and committed our lives to Jesus Christ. With all our hearts we sincerely wanted to serve the Lord in any way He saw fit.

It was about that time that a counselor from our church told us about a boy named Chris. He was seven years old and needed a place to stay for the weekend. His father had recently remarried and was having some marriage problems. Chris, through no problem of his own, seemed to be caught in the middle of their problems. The counselor asked if we would be willing to take Chris home with us for the weekend. In the meantime, his dad and stepmother would have some time to work on their marriage issues.

We had a big house and my wife said she was willing to find room for him. Yvonne, our kids, and I prayed about it. After prayer, we all agreed it seemed to us the right thing to do. I called the counselor and told him that we were willing as long as his dad told Chris that he would be staying with us for the weekend and why he was visiting us. I felt that it would help Chris understand his family situation and understand that it had to do with adult issues and wasn't his fault.

We met Chris and his father at the church parking lot. His father handed him a couple of paper grocery bags full of clothes and said goodbye. Chris looked up at me through those dark-rimmed glasses of his. He was a little kid then and all I could see was those big, dark- rimmed glasses. I told him, "Chris you're coming home with us for the weekend. Let's go get in the car." I introduced him to Yvonne and the kids and away we went.

We had about a half-hour ride home from the church. On the way, I learned that his dad had not told him he would be staying with us for the weekend or why he was with us. I figured that I had better tell Chris that he would be staying with us for the weekend in order to give his dad and stepmother some time to work things out. That was OK with him. He was already making friends with our children.

We got a call from the counselor late Sunday night asking if Chris could stay for a week. His dad would call in and make arrangements with us to pick him up. As it turned out, he didn't call for a few weeks.

He and his wife continued to have problems.

Chris had settled into our home and family and was going to school. We heard from Chris's father off and on and occasionally he visited Chris during the next few years. His mother visited him once in awhile. Both of his parents were always welcome at our house. We had a pleasant time with them when they came to visit Chris.

My wife taught Chris that the Bible teaches us to honor our mother and father. He didn't have to agree with their lifestyle, but he must be respectful toward both of them. God promises us a long life if we honor our parents. It's the only commandment with a promise. She taught him to honor us as well, because we were the parents God gave him for this part of his life.

A few years after Chris came to live with us, we got a call from his father asking if we could take his other son, Joe, who was two years older than Chris. He and his wife were still having marital problems. I talked with Yvonne and our children and we all prayed about it. We all agreed that brothers should be together if at all possible. Yvonne and I are close to our brothers, and we felt Chris and Joe should have a chance to be together. His dad brought Joe over a few days later. Joe had a few more problems than Chris but they didn't seem too serious.

Joe was tall and slender and very quiet. He soon learned to talk and laugh with all of us. He loved cooking and would cook up some dishes that didn't always look good, but usually tasted good. He seemed to get along with the other kids and they all had some good times together. He had a few problems that we had to address early on. He enjoyed the young people's Bible Study at the youth pastor's home and always looked forward to youth meetings at our church, Scholls Community Church. The meetings were a priority for him.

By this time our sons, Don and Steve, were in college. Don attended Southern Oregon State College in Ashland, Oregon, and Steve attended Le Tourneau University in Longview, Texas. The younger children enjoyed having Don and Steve come home during breaks and summer vacations.

Billie Jean was ten years old and our two adopted children were seven and eight. They were all good kids and were such a blessing to me. Now they weren't perfect, but my wife and I didn't experience the problems and heartache that so many of our friends and coworkers did.

Things went well over the years, and soon Chris was fourteen years old and Joe was sixteen. They were old enough to go hunting with me. Yvonne took them to hunter safety classes in Hillsboro. They learned a lot about gun safety, hunting, emergencies, and survival skills in the wilderness.

We were ready for a big hunting trip! I had gone on

many hunting trips with my hunting buddy, Chuck. We had good times and always got our deer or elk. We hunted all over the state of Oregon. We cooked our food over an open campfire and it tasted so good!

CHAPTER TWO

"IT'S SNOWING IN THE MOUNTAINS"

*The heavens will praise Your
wonders, O Lord*

Psalm 89:5

How many of you know that the Lord is always looking out for you and guiding your path? If you don't know now, you will know by the time you finish reading this story. It all happened to me. I am going to tell you a true story about how the Lord provided for my two boys and me on our elk hunting trip in the rugged mountains of Oregon, on November 21, 1978.

It was early in the morning and the kids were bustling around the house getting ready for the day. The older ones were helping Yvonne get breakfast ready. Joe was making pancakes, Chris was frying bacon, and I was scrambling eggs. The girls were setting the dining room table. The children using the bathroom would finish washing and brushing their teeth and come out to the kitchen. They would relieve those preparing breakfast, so they could get washed and ready to eat.

My wife insisted that all the children come to the table with their faces washed and hair combed. She told them that they were all going to be leaders and must come to the dining room table neat and clean and learn proper table manners.

The phone rang. It was my hunting partner and Christian friend, Chuck. "Let's go hunting!" He added that it was snowing on the mountain and it would be easier to see the elk.

"What a great day to hunt elk!" I said. " Ok. I'll get the boys and be over to pick you up."

Then I thought about the trip ahead. We had been hunting the weekend before in the pouring rain. We all got soaking wet and were chilled clear to the bone.

On top of that we had not even seen a sign of elk, not even any tracks. I said, "I don't know."

Chuck quickly replied, "We only have this weekend and next, then elk season is over for this year."

"Ok," I said, "As soon as the boys and I are ready, we'll be over to pick you up." It wasn't hard to talk me into hunting. and I knew the boys would be ready to go hunting at a moment's notice!

I asked Chuck," Did you talk to your wife about this? She's been a little upset about you going hunting so often." He answered, "I really did some talking. It took more than a half hour before she reluctantly agreed to let me go hunting again this weekend."

I'll bet he had to make some promises to stay in her good graces. He didn't tell me about that.

Hey, wait a minute, in all the excitement, I forgot to make sure it was okay with Yvonne. I put my hand over the receiver, "It's Chuck and he wants to know if we can go hunting with him today."

Yvonne said, "We who?"

"Joe, Chris and me," I replied.

" I guess it's okay if you bring home an elk."

"Do you mind if we finish breakfast first?" I took my hand off the receiver and said, "I'll get the boys and be over to pick you up as soon as we eat breakfast. Yvonne made me promise we would bring home an elk."

I told the boys, Chris and Joe, to get ready. Joe was sixteen years old and weighed about a hundred and twenty pounds. He stood about five feet nine inches tall. He had dark hair and brown eyes. He was full of energy and always on the move. He was at the age when he thought that girls were pretty nice, but if he had to choose between girls and hunting, he would choose hunting.

Chris was fourteen years old, was five feet six inches tall, and weighed about a hundred thirty pounds. He had thick dark hair and brown eyes. His favorite sport was riding trail bikes. We had a year around creek flowing through our land and he liked to play in the creek.

One year the beavers built a dam in the creek and flooded about an acre of our land. That made a nice pond for fish and for the kids to swim in during the summer months and skate on during the winter. He spent his extra time swimming and playing in the creek with the other kids. He was a pleasant addition to our family and was always ready for a good practical joke.

"Boys, get ready we're going elk hunting. It's snowing in the mountains. Come on, hurry up, let's get moving." We knew it would be easier to track elk in the snow.

You can't believe how quickly the boys got ready. There was a flurry of coats, vests, stocking caps! On went our warmest hunting jackets. "Where are my gloves?" "Have you seen my cap?" "Mom, what did you do with my boots?" "I found my old ones, but I still can't find my new ones." "Oh well, I will wear my old ones. We're just going for the day." "Have you seen my gloves?"

It was chaos, but there was order amidst all the chaos!

My youngest son, who was eight at the time, said, "When I get old enough, I want to go with you. I hope you bag an elk, Dad."

I yelled over my shoulder, "We will, we will, son."

In no time at all the boys had all their gear in the truck and were standing at the door waiting for me. I didn't realize at the time that Chris had his old boots on and they had a hole in them.

Chris and Joe had completed National Rifle Association Hunter Safety School in Hillsboro, Oregon. We lived about fourteen miles from Hillsboro. Yvonne drove them to the classes. She had to take all the younger children with her. It was quite a car full! They looked forward to each class and learned lots of new information. They became quite knowledgeable about everything related to hunter safety.

They would take turns sharing all the things they learned while we were having dinner. First, Joe would ask me a question, then it was Chris' turn to ask the question. They would quiz me to see if I knew the answers. Most of the time, I wasn't quite sure of the answer. They would chuckle and say, "Dad you better go to hunter safety class with us."

I would let them know I had to work. "If we want food on the table, I have to work."

They would laughingly say, "That's OK dad, we will teach you." They prided themselves on being careful to follow all the safety rules they had learned.

Joe's rifle was a 30.6 semi-automatic with a 4/10 scope on it. He bought it at a sale. It was in good shape. Chris was using my son Steven's rifle. It was a 30.6 with a 4/10 scope on it. It was fairly new. Steven gave him permission to use it as long as he didn't put a scratch on it. My rifle was a German

Mauser drilled out for a 3/08. It had a scope on it. We had carrying cases for all of our rifles.

Amid the flurry, Billie Jean, my ten-year-old daughter, spoke up, "Why can't I go, Daddy? "I want to go hunting with you too. I won't be any trouble daddy, I promise, I promise."

I reached down and gave her a big hug, reminding her that when she got a little older she would have to go to hunter safety school. Then, if she still wanted to, she could go hunting with me.

My two younger children weren't too interested in hunting yet. They were getting ready to go outside and build a snowman. They were putting on boots, gloves and their warm coats. They were scurrying around trying to feel as important as the mighty hunters. "Mom, we need a scarf and a hat for our snowman. What should we use for his eyes and his mouth?"

We checked all our gear out carefully: guns, ammunition, candy bars, tree sap for starting a fire and water. To show you how the Lord takes care of us, the tree sap that we had was from a hunting trip that we had taken earlier in the year.

Joe and I were sitting at a deer stand waiting and watching for the deer. We had been sitting there for a long time. He noticed a pine tree just a few feet to the left of us. Joe said, "Dad, do you see all the sap coming out of that pine tree over there? Would it be alright if I got some of it?"

I replied, "It sounds like a good idea to me, but what are you going to put it in?"

Joe thought about that for awhile. "Remember the chocolate chip cookies Mom made for us? Should we eat them and use the plastic bags they are in to collect the sap?"

I wasn't quite sure what was more important to Joe, eating the cookies or collecting the sap. Well, we both enjoyed eating those chocolate chip cookies. We made fast work of them!

Joe took the bags and his hunting knife, cut the sap off the tree and put it in the plastic bags. He filled them as full as he could get them. When he came back to the stand, he said, "You know Dad, this sap is good for starting fires. When we get home, I'll make a bag for each of us and put matches in. I'll put them in our backpacks."

I sarcastically thought to myself, yeah, like we'll ever use it. Who knows! Maybe we will!

Yes, our gear was all there. Some of it was still in the truck from our hunt the previous weekend. It had rained so hard that we couldn't even find any tracks. We all came home soaking wet. We were familiar with that. We lived in Oregon. No one complained.

Joe yelled to anyone listening, "Hey you guys, I put that sap and some matches in our packs." The boys were busy checking their backpacks. They loved the outdoors and hunting as much as Chuck and I did. We had many good times hunting all over the state of Oregon.

I had just bought a four-wheel drive and I wanted to see what it would do in the snow. I knew that it was going to be a lot of fun! It was a '73 GMC four-wheel drive with a big winch on the front of it. Anyone who hunts in Oregon needs a winch on the truck.

The roads we traveled to get to our hunting spot were all mud with big ruts. It was necessary to have at least fifty feet of cable on the winch. When we got stuck we would unroll the cable from the winch, and pull the cable out as far as we could go. Then we look for the biggest tree close to the road. We would wrap the cable to the tree at the base and start up the winch and gas up the truck. Most of the time this would get us out of the rut. Sometimes it would be necessary to do this several times before reaching our campsite.

By the time we got to our campsite, we were all covered with mud. We knew this would happen, so we would always make sure that we had a big tarp over our trailer that we pulled behind the four-wheeler. We would have the tarp fastened down real tight. That way our camping gear and supplies didn't get covered with mud. By the time we got to our camping site, we were worn out from just trying to get there. We would unload the trailer and one of us would stay at the campsite.

The rest of us would drive the truck and trailer out to get wood for the campfire. We would take our chain saws and a can of gas and go out until we found a big tree that had fallen down. Often it would be lying amongst other dead brush. That's when our winch would come in handy again. We would find a clear spot as close as possible to the tree. We would park the truck there, pull out the winch, wrap it around the tree, and pull the tree out of the brush into the clear spot. This made it easier to cut the tree up with the chain saw. We loaded the wood on the trailer and returned to the campsite.

Upon returning to the campsite, we would split the wood and build a fire. We would find rock, as big as we could carry and form a circle of rocks for the fire pit. Soon we would have a nice, warm fire going. Our next project was setting up camp. Our goal was to get all of this done before dark on the first day. We would go out one or two days before hunting season started to set up camp. We would scout out the highest spot around so we would be sitting in it when the sun came up the first day of hunting season.

We all had layers of warm clothes on and out the door we went! As I hurried out the door, I gave my wife a quick smooch on the cheek. She said, "Get back here, I want a real kiss." I didn't mind obliging her one bit. The boys, already halfway to the truck, yelled, "Goodbye, Mom." She reminded us to be careful as she closed the door and turned to tend to the younger children.

In no time at all we were in the truck heading for Chuck's house. We picked up Chuck, loaded all his gear and headed for the mountain. Chuck was about five feet seven and weighed in at about a hundred fifty pounds. He worked in the ship yards in Portland as an electrician. He made pretty good money. His equipment was the best you could buy. He had a 300 Savage with a large scope and had a powerful spotting scope, as well.

The closer we got to the mountain, the harder it was snowing. The snow was falling in those big, soft flakes that make you want to be out in it. It always makes me feel like a kid again. When we got to the guard shack, we were asked where we planned to hunt. We had to get a pass because we were hunting on private land. It was a large paper company's tree farm.

The guard gave us a card that was numbered. We had to sign our names and write the number of the card next to each name. We were to give it back to him when we came back out to the gate. That way they know that all hunters are out before they close and lock the gate.

As we drove up the mountain, we could see that all the trucks were going the opposite way. For some reason, they were all leaving. The closer we got to the mountain, the more it snowed. That should have told us something.

Chuck and I looked at each other and I said, "What do you think?"

He replied, "Let's go on up to the big mill pond and look around for tracks. If we don't find any, we'll head back."

Finding no tracks at the pond, we started to head back down the mountain. The snow was a couple feet deep and it was a little slippery by this time. My new four-wheeler had no trouble in the snow.

CHAPTER THREE

WHITEOUT

And I will wait on Your name, for it is good...

Psalm 52:9

Joe spotted an open meadow with trees around it. I was pretty enthusiastic and I yelled, "Hey, Chuck, why don't we stop here. It looks like a good place to make a push around behind the meadow and try to drive the elk out of the trees." We all decided that Chuck would take the open spot near the truck and watch for the elk as they came out of the woods. The boys and I would make the drive.

Chuck quickly responded, "Yeh, let's do it!" None of us were ready to quit yet, even though it was snowing pretty hard.

The boys and I got our backpacks and guns out of the truck and headed into the woods. Later, I realized that in all the excitement, we had forgotten to pick up our walkie-talkies with the rest of our gear. We were laughing and talking excitedly as we walked in the newly fallen snow. It made crunchy sounds with our every step.

I was checking for landmarks to make sure we would come out the same way we went in. I saw a group of trees that were not quite as tall and their trunks were smaller than the other trees around them. They were growing in an almost perfect and very large semi-circle. I knew without any misgiving that I would not miss them on our way out. They stood out in striking contrast to everything around them.

We walked for quite awhile and before we knew it, a whiteout began to move in. I had seen whiteouts in Alaska, but I was in the city of Fairbanks and pretty close to home. There were buildings and people all around, but out here in the middle of nowhere it was a different story. It was a lonely feeling, but the boys and I were having a good time telling each other stories. The boys were telling me the things they had learned in hunter safety class and it was quite interesting. They had picked up a lot of good information. I was pleased that they had taken such an interest in the class and remembered so much.

It wasn't very long until we realized that we had lost all sense of direction. It was impossible to see where we were going. You couldn't see your hand in front of you. We stayed close together and knew that we had to stop and wait for the whiteout to pass. We reluctantly sat down and waited for it to stop. We protected ourselves by sitting next to a huge log under a tree. The branches were thick and there wasn't much snow beneath the tree. The whiteout seemed like it lasted for hours. According to my watch it really lasted about twenty minutes. It seemed like an awfully long time to us.

We all three prayed that God would protect us. Chris said that we should pray for Chuck, too. I'm not sure I prayed with a sincere attitude because I was still very sure of myself. It wouldn't take me long to know that I had better put my confidence in the Lord.

My son, Steve, who was a bush pilot in Alaska for quite a few years, told me that when he is flying an aircraft during whiteout conditions he must depend on the instruments. He said that it is a very real possibility that he may lose all sense of direction. Alaskan bush pilots have lost their lives during whiteouts from loss of their sense of direction.

Steven graduated from LeTourneau University in Longview, Texas with a degree in Aeronautical Science and Business. During his summer breaks he flew for airlines in Alaska. He flew for airlines out of Tok, Galena, Fairbanks and some other places.

By the way, Steven was one of the best and most dependable bush pilots to fly the perilous Alaskan skies. The Native Alaskans called him "Bushman." He wore his thick, dark hair a little too long for me and grew a full beard. In the dead of the Alaskan winter he looked like a true Bushman!

I've talked to Steven about writing a book about his experiences in the Alaskan Bush. He responded by saying, "No one would believe it!"

I admire his courage and am a proud dad. His mother says that he made her a woman of prayer during the years he was a bush pilot. She would get so worried about him that she would almost panic.

She would go to her room, get on her knees and put him in the hands of the Lord. When she told Steven that she was concerned about him, he would have a good hearty laugh, say that he was fine, and ask her why she worried so much.

I'm very proud of my son, Don, as well. He is a fine young man. During his second year in college he hunted with a bow and successfully bagged his deer. He says the deer at least has a chance when he is hunting with the bow. He dressed out the deer, packaged it and put it in the freezer. He had enough meat for the rest of the school year. Don is a college graduate and has his Master's Degree in Business from Northern Arizona University. He is a professor at Regis University in Denver. He was selected Instructor of the *Year* by his peers and the students two years in a row.

When the weather let up, we decided to head back toward the truck. The whiteout disoriented me and I couldn't find any of my landmarks. About this time I was thinking about how I plunge into things and often don't even think of what the outcome will be. I knew that I needed to make some changes in my life. I tend to rush through life and forget to slow down and enjoy the moment I am in. I've learned in life that there is a lesson to be learned through everything that happens to us. I need to stop and listen to God, and He will show me the way. He will give me direction.

My problem is sometimes I don't stop and listen. I forge right on ahead. When all else fails and I am in big trouble, I ask for help. One of these days I will ask Him for guidance sooner. It sure would make my life simpler and easier. It would save those around me a lot of pain and anguish, as well. My family is the most important thing I have and they can be taken away from me quickly.

One of the things I learned in my childhood was how to take care of myself in difficult circumstances. I had to provide for myself many times. That meant, if there was no food, I had to find something to eat. If there wasn't any way to cook it, I had to get a fire going. I learned a lot about wood and what kind to use to get a fire going. I figured out what kind burns hot. I knew that pitch was found in the center of dead logs and at the point where the branch grows out of the trunk of the tree.

The combination of the things I learned in my youth the hard way and everything the boys learned in hunter safety school saved our lives that long, dark night the three of us spent in the *Hell Hole*. We started walking one way, but again, nothing seemed right, so we turned around and walked the other way. What I should have done at this point was stop, pray, and ask God for direction. I had been teaching our church youth group from Proverbs. Looking back, I can't help but think of Proverbs 28:26: "He who trusts in his own heart is a fool, but he who walks wisely will be delivered."

Joe felt that he was getting too far from us and might get lost, so he started walking with me. Chris saw Joe and me walking together, so he decided to join us. As we walked on down the hill, we heard a noise and I thought I saw something. We stopped at a large log so I could lay my rifle across it and look through my scope. I looked all around where we had heard the noise but I couldn't see a thing.

The boys had their rifles ready and were looking through their scopes. They didn't see anything either. We were all sure we had heard the movement of animals in the woods. We stayed at that log for quite awhile. It became apparent that whatever we heard either wasn't an elk or hadn't come our way. I don't know how true it is, but I've always said the animals seem to know when the hunter is in the woods.

We watched and listened, but much to our disappointment we didn't hear or see anything. We stayed at the log and chatted for about half an hour. We always seemed to have plenty to talk about. When we were rested up, we started down the hill again, but this time we stayed together. This was not the time to be separated.

It was starting to cloud over more heavily, and because of the heavy snowfall it was getting harder to see. I wasn't worried. I knew we would find the road soon. As soon as we got to the road, we would walk right back to the truck. Chuck would be at the truck and then we would decide what we were going to do. We might hunt for a while longer or we might decide to go home. We all loved to be out in the woods hunting. We didn't give up our hunt easily.

Unbeknown to us at the time, the farther we walked, the farther we got from the road that would lead us back to our truck. I was getting a little concerned until we found footprints in the snow. We decided to follow them, thinking that surely they would lead us back to a road, any road. By now the boys and I just wanted to get back to the truck. We followed the footprints down an unusually steep hill, but after a mile or so the prints led us back up the hill.

We stopped there and I told the boys that we should leave the footprints and go on down the hill. I really didn't want to walk up that big hill, and I was sure that we would find the road at the bottom of the hill. We started down the hill, not knowing that we were entering what hunters had named the *Hell Hole*. We would learn later that hunters had named this treacherous place for good reason. There was only one way in and one way out.

After awhile we ran onto a very old logging road. It was pretty well grown over with brush, but it was easier walking so we stayed on it. We walked for a short time and it ran out too. I knew at this moment that we were lost. Joe gave me that knowing look. We didn't want to discourage Chris so we didn't say a word. Whenever I get myself into any kind of trouble I ask my best friend, Jesus, to help me out and He always does. In Hebrews 13:5: He tells us, "I will never leave you or forsake you." He has never failed me.

Going down it was a steep hill; walking back up, it was a steep mountain! The snow and ice with jagged rocks underneath made it difficult to climb. We kept on walking and climbing in the direction that we thought would take us back to the truck. Sounds like the way we live our lives. Proverbs 14:12: "There is a way which seems right to a man, but its end is the way of death."

It was beginning to get dark and I was worried. I finally gave up my pride and prayed: "Lord, I'm lost and I don't know where to go or what to do. What should I do, Lord? What's going to happen to the boys and me? We're in Your hands!" It wasn't easy to give up my pride and admit that I made a mistake. After all I had hunted in so many different terrains in many different places and had never been lost. How could I get lost?

CHAPTER FOUR

FINDING A CAMPSITE

*He only is my rock and my
salvation, my stronghold, I shall not
be greatly shaken.*

Psalm 62:2

What should we do? I needed desperately to look to the Lord for answers. I didn't pray out loud as I didn't want to alarm the boys. They were good boys and were respectful of Mom and me. We enjoyed them and felt that God gave us the blessing of raising them. We knew their birth parents really missed out. Early on in my Christian walk I began reading a chapter of Proverbs every day. We tried to be good parents to them. I asked God to give me wisdom to raise all my children. I didn't want anything to happen to Chris and Joe.

Just as I finished my prayer, Joe said, "Dad, in hunting school they taught us to follow our tracks back." Was I glad that I sent them to hunting school! We turned and started following our footsteps back. I soon realized that I had waited too long. My pride was in the way. Pride is never our friend. Pride is a thief and a cheater. If we allow it, pride will cheat us out of everything God has planned for us.

I didn't want my hunting buddy of many years to think William Bush would get lost. Chuck, my boys, and I had enjoyed many hunting trips together all over the beautiful state of Oregon. We had never been lost or even come close to getting lost. We all had the best gear we needed, including a good compass.

We had gone a long ways, much farther than I had

initially thought. We had waited too long and gone too far. It was getting dark and we couldn't go any farther. We couldn't see our footprints anyway. Fear was beginning to fill our minds, making it difficult to think clearly. The cold, stormy weather and fear don't make a good combination.

Again, Joe said, "In our hunter safety class they told us to stop about a half hour before dark, find a campsite, get a fire going, and gather wood for the night."

"Sure, sure," I thought, "where will we find wood? We're walking in at least two feet of snow. Even if we can find wood, it will be covered with snow and won't burn. How will we find the wood? It's dark and everything is covered with a lot of snow."

I was making excuses because I didn't want to stop. I wanted to keep going and get out of this place. We were all beginning to get a little cold. The boys were using good common sense. That nagging feeling that I had to get us out of there and back home kept me going.

I knew Mom and the younger kids were probably all in front of the nice warm fireplace, expecting us home any minute. She would have some good home-cooked food ready for us to eat the minute we stepped in the door. I could almost smell the bread baking in the oven. She would say what she always told us, "Don't make a mess, you guys."

Chris and Joe found three campsites and showed me each one. Each site had pros and cons. By the time we looked at the third site, it was almost dark. I finally had to accept that we were not getting out that night. Our best chance seemed to be to try to settle in as best we could for the night. It was the best site anyway. It was almost dark by this time, and let me tell you it is dark out in those woods. The mountain is no place to be after dark, especially if you're lost and scared.

The boys and I realized that our situation was bad and getting worse by the minute. The boys were scared and so was I. We couldn't let fear cloud our thinking. What should we do? Chris and Joe kept telling me what they felt we should do. I was half listening, and thinking about our situation. What is the best way out? Which direction should we go? The boys were taught in their hunter safety classes that if you are lost and have to spend the night in the woods, you should find a place that will protect you from the bad weather, in our case a snowstorm. It is best to stop at least a half hour before dark and find a place to spend the night as well as gather firewood. Often hunters try to keep going and they become exhausted and freeze to death.

I wanted to keep going as far as possible, so we pushed on. I thought sure we would get out that night, and I didn't want my friends to know that I had been lost in the woods. I was letting my pride get in the way of my good judgment again.

Chris and Joe found another place to spend the night. It was a little off the trail we had been on and I felt completely at ease about it. A huge fallen log about a hundred feet long and five feet high formed one side. The other side was protected by a log about ten feet long and three feet high. Another log and a mound of dirt partially protected the other sides. Together these formed an ideal protected spot. Or at least it was about as ideal as being lost in a snowstorm overnight can be.

I had to swallow my pride and give in. I realized that we were not going to get out that night. The best thing to do was to start a fire and wait. We decided to fire three shots up in the air, hoping that my hunting partner would hear and answer. We each fired a shot and that probably wasn't the best thing to do. Our rifles were different calibers. As a result, my partner thought we were firing on elk and didn't answer our shots.

Chuck had decided that he would walk out to the guard shack when hunters in a jeep stopped to talk with him. He told them about the situation and that the boys and I hadn't come back to the truck. They had heard a herd of elk running across the road, and right after that they heard our shots. They assumed that we were shooting at the elk.

Failing to get an answer from our shots, we set

about gathering wood for the night. We began to break the little branches off the bottoms of the trees. The branches were covered with ice and snow, so we broke them up as small as we could.

How do you start a fire with snow-covered wood? We used the pitch Joe had saved. He had put matches in each bag of pitch. If he had not done this, we would not have had any way to start a fire. None of us smoke and we never carry matches.

We made a pile of the smallest sticks we could find. We looked in our pockets and wallets for any pieces of paper we could use to get a fire going. All we could find were some bills in my wallet. Not having much choice, even though it was difficult for me, I crumpled some of my bills and put them under the wood, leaving plenty of air space and hoping that we could get a fire going. I took the pack of pitch and matches out of my vest and lit the pile. The wood was just too wet and wouldn't catch. After awhile it started burning, but just barely. It was difficult to watch those bills burn! I was pretty careful with my money and the word "wasteful" was not in my vocabulary.

It was getting dark fast, the wood was wet, I was getting cold and the boys were colder. The fire was spitting and sputtering and refusing to burn. I was pretty frustrated by this time. I fussed with the fire, trying to get it going, but things didn't look very good for us. I told the boys that I didn't think we were ever going to get a fire going.

Chris just looked at me and said, "Well Dad, you always taught us to pray about things."

"Why don't we ask the Lord to get the fire going," Joe added.

I was still pretty frustrated over my failure to start the fire. I said, "We sure need to do something."

At the boys' insistence, we stood around the fire and held hands. We all fervently prayed, asking God to take care of the fire. God answered our prayers almost instantly. No sooner had we prayed and opened our eyes than the fire flared right up! It burned so bright that we could see a lot better and we were able to gather quite a bit of wood. We gathered more wood but it was all covered with ice and snow. Each time we put some of it on the fire, it would begin sputtering and almost go out. Every time the fire began to sputter and go out, we would join hands around it and pray, believing God would answer our urgent prayers. Immediately after our prayers, the fire would flare right up and burn warm and bright.

By this time it was getting bitterly cold. We were cold, but we had a fire going. Our thoughts turned to our hunting partner, Chuck. I knew he would be waiting back at the truck for us. He wouldn't be able to get in the truck because I had the keys. Why didn't I leave the keys on the front tire, as we always did? What was I thinking? Was I thinking at all? He wouldn't be able to get in the truck and stay warm. The boys and I prayed to the Lord, asking Him to keep Chuck safe and warm and not let him freeze. After we prayed, we knew that our good friend, Chuck, was safely in the hands of God.

Feeling confident that the Lord was taking care of Chuck, we turned our attention back to the fire. It was burning a lot better now, but we knew that we would have to find some bigger pieces of wood or the fire would not last the night. We had to devise a better method to gather the wood. Everything was covered with so much snow. What we decided to do was go out as far from the fire as we could. Except for the fire, it was pitch black in those woods. We would shuffle our feet around until we kicked something. Next we would bring it closer to the fire, hoping it was wood. This is the way we gathered our wood for the night.

When we got the fire going good enough to see out a ways, Joe decided that he was going to build us a lean-to. The cold November winds whistled through the tops of the tall pine trees and seemed to go right through us. It was an eerie sound at times. All we had was the hatchet on Joe's belt. He went out to cut some small trees for the lean-to. On the first swing, the hatchet flew right out of his hand and into the snow. We looked for it in the deep snow for quite awhile, but never did find it. The only branches we could use were the ones we could break off by hand.

We had built the fire by the log that was about three feet high. We had a pretty good fire going by this time. The smoke from it was billowing up over the log, and the snow and ice on the log were melting. I realized that where the smoke goes, most of the heat goes. We began putting the logs with snow and ice on them on the three-foot-high log and when the snow and ice melted off them, we put them on the fire. As a result, the fire burned much hotter all night.

When I came back from gathering another load of wood, I noticed that the rifles were frosted over. A closer look convinced me they were frozen. They were only three feet from the fire. At that moment in time I realized how cold it was in this snow-covered Oregon wilderness in the middle of the night. I figured that I would move them closer to the fire. I reached out and grabbed the barrel of my gun, but my hand stuck to it and I couldn't get it off. I had to lean over the fire with that rifle stuck to my hand and warm up the gun before I could get my hand loose without losing a lot of skin in the process. I fully realized how serious our situation was. I couldn't help but think of Joe and Chris and their well being. Oh, how I prayed for their safety.

The entire night went this way. There was one life-threatening situation after another. Every time I looked at my watch, it seemed time moved slower and slower. I wasn't sure if it was going slow because of the cold. I had to keep us all awake. If we fell asleep, the situation could get worse. I felt that if we kept moving, our circulation would improve and we would stay warmer.

We had to forage for wood most of that night to keep the fire built up so we could stay warm. In between trips for wood, we talked about a lot of things and we prayed off and on. We talked about how we had goofed up and wound up here in the first place. We talked seriously about how we could use all of our survival skills.

Men and boys don't always say a lot, but let me tell you, we did a lot of talking. I didn't want the boys to get discouraged. "It's important for us to have hope and not give up," I said.

Joe commented, "Even though we can't ever give up our hope, we should always be prepared to die."

I mentioned to them, "Maybe we should make a plan."

"We're all Christians, so is there anything else we need to do?" Chris asked.

"I think that it is important for all three of us to

admit our sins and ask God to forgive us," I answered.

"I am so cold, Dad, my feet are so cold," Chris said quietly. Chris realized that in his rush to get going, he had put on his old pair of boots. One of them had a hole in the bottom, causing his feet to get cold. Joe and I kept him as close as possible to the fire and didn't let him gather wood. By this time we had a blazing fire.

We agreed that we would confess our sins to each other and we would ask God to forgive us. I remembered the verse that goes something like this: If we confess our sins, He is faithful and just to forgive us and cleanse us from all unrighteousness.

Joe said, "I feel so much better now."

Chris added, "I sure needed that."

I needed God's forgiveness too. We all do.

We all admitted to doing some things that we shouldn't have done. We believed with all our hearts that the Lord would bring us out of this ordeal safely. We remembered home and family. All through that long, dark night we encouraged each other as we gathered wood to keep the fire going.

By this time we were all getting quite hungry. We checked our vest pockets and found three candy bars, three of Mom's homemade chocolate chip cookies, three boxes of raisins, and one strip of red licorice. The licorice was melting due to our wet clothes. We laid the licorice out in the snow to harden it. We decided that we would each eat one candy bar and save the rest of our food for the next day. We ate our candy bars slowly and believe me, I never knew a candy bar could taste so good.

We were concerned about Mom and the younger kids. I couldn't help but ask myself what could I have done to prevent this from happening. It was too late to think about that right now. Chris and Joe were depending on me and I must not let them down. It was my job to keep them safe and alive. I was confident that Jesus would never let us down. He would never let any of my children down.

God was teaching us through this harsh experience. I know that He doesn't allow anything to happen in our lives without a purpose. Even the foolish things we do. He will turn it around and help us learn. Only the Lord could help us now.

At this point I had to use all of the survival skills I had learned in my growing up years to survive the trial we were going through. I stopped and prayed, "Lord, what can I do to get us safely back to the truck?" The thought came to my mind: *Son, I will never leave you or forsake you.* It must have been from the Lord because I felt much more at ease. I knew that somehow, some way, we were going to get out of this! I began to feel better and my strength was renewed.

I began to think of life in general and how I could have done so many things differently. I started to think of myself and remember my own life, but it came to mind that I needed to stop thinking of myself and instead think of the two boys with me. I began to concentrate on what was best for them and how I could get them home safely. They needed my comfort and encouragement.

I moved over to where Chris and Joe were sitting and began talking to them. I said, "Remember our last hunting trip? We were sitting in the tent and it was pouring down rain. The only place that the tent leaked was right over where I was sitting. You guys were laughing pretty hard because I was the only one getting wet!" They both laughed again as they remembered. Joe said, "Yeh, and remember that you were so stubborn that you got your army poncho out, put it on, and just sat there in the rain!"

I sure couldn't deny that! I could see how stubbornness has been a big problem for me. I was taking a good look at myself.

Chris reminded us how warm it was inside the tent. We had a pretty big tent, twenty by twenty and seven feet tall. It was big enough for a stove and cots and all of our gear. It was cold and rainy outside but warm and comfortable inside the tent.

My hunting partner brought his camper on the back of his truck so we could cook on the stove in his camper if we wanted to. Sometimes it was pretty slow cooking on the wood stove.

The first few times we went hunting, Chris and Joe would listen to Chuck and me swap stories. After a few hunting trips, they started to jump right in with their stories. They probably figured that not all the stories were true. Some parts were true and some made up, so they decided they could do that! It was a good time of fellowship and getting to know each other better.

Sometimes we talked about school and things that were bothering them. Joe said, " I have problems getting all my schoolwork done because I don't pay enough attention in class." He went on to say, "I wish I would have paid more attention to what I learned in hunter safety class. If I would have listened, I would have brought all my gear with me instead of leaving it in the truck."

Chris spoke up, "That goes for me too, but you're the oldest and you should have thought of it."

Joe replied, "At least I was smart enough to wear boots without a hole in them!"

We had a good laugh and went back to our task of gathering wood for the fire.

Once in awhile we talked about things that bothered us about each other! Friendships were discussed and the types of friends they associated with. They wondered why their parents hadn't kept their family together. They questioned why it was difficult to like some people. All in all it was a good time for them to open up and get things off their chests.

We always looked forward to our hunting trips. The boys knew that if they didn't keep their grades in school up, they would not be allowed to go with me.

Joe reminisced about the good food that I cooked for us on those hunting trips. He said, "I remember the night you made steak and brussel sprouts with cheese sauce. Mmm, that was good! Later on you made us hot chocolate. I sure wish we had some of that hot chocolate right now."

Chris and I answered together, "So do I."

I asked the boys, "What were some of the best times you had on our hunting trips?"

Chris said, "The time I laughed the hardest was on an elk hunting trip to Eastern Oregon." He, Joe and Chuck were walking down a dirt road talking, with their rifles slung over their shoulders. They hadn't seen anything all day so they had sort of given up for the day.

Joe said, "All of a sudden up over the bank and

across the road came this four-point buck. We were only about a hundred yards away from it."

They all brought their guns around. Chuck had just gotten a bead on the elk when Joe fired off a shot. It scared Chuck so much that he couldn't even pull the trigger. Chris just stood there with his mouth wide open. Chuck was so upset and jarred from the blast so close to his ear that he had to sit down on a rock to calm himself down. Joe said, "The look on his face was something else and I knew I shouldn't have laughed, but I couldn't control it."

Apparently Joe missed completely or hit the elk where it didn't slow him down. We walked up the hill where we had seen the elk run. We followed the elk prints for about an hour but didn't see any blood. The elk was nowhere in sight, so we headed back toward camp.

Chuck told us later that night that when Joe fired off that shot, it scared him so bad he peed his pants. He related that he was concentrating so completely on that elk that he forgot anyone else was around. When Joe fired off his shot so close to his ear, it scared him. Chuck told Joe later, "Wait till I tell your dad, the only elk we saw all week and you missed it."

Later that evening, Joe shared, " Now I understand what you mean about buck fever, Dad." He recounted that when he saw that elk, all he could think was shoot it. He said that he didn't even aim. He just raised his rifle and fired. For a moment, he forgot all he had learned in hunter safety classes. He just wanted that elk.

Chris recounted that when we got home from a hunt, it was so much fun to gather at Chuck's house and dress the deer or elk out. Mom, Chuck's wife, and all the younger kids would be there to help. Dad and Chuck carefully cut the roasts, ribs, steaks, and stew meat. Then Mom and Chuck's wife would wrap the meat in freezer paper. They would hold it and one of the kids would tape it. Everyone talked and laughed while they worked. It was family time and it was fun! When we were finished, we divided up the meat, and both families had plenty of meat for the winter.

Chris said, "Dad, remember the fishing trip we went on?"

I thought to myself, if the boys still want to talk, the fishing trip would be a good subject. It would help pass the time faster and take their minds off our situation, as well. One day a friend of mine from work came to me and said, "Bill, I just bought a new boat and would like to go out deep sea fishing. Would you and your two boys like to go with me?"

I said, "That sounds good. When would you like to go?"

"How about in two weeks, on the sixteenth?" I had known Ken for quite some time and he was a good, dependable guy.

I checked it out with my wife and she told me we didn't have anything planned for that date. The boys' schedule was clear, as well. I thanked him for inviting the boys and me on the fishing trip. I had been deep sea fishing many times. My company took all the foreman and supervisors fishing each year. The boat was larger than Ken's and accommodated more people. I thoroughly enjoyed each excursion and looked forward to this one.

Ken's boat was big enough to go over the bar safely. Going over the Columbia River bar can be very rough. The river is more than four miles wide as it pours into the Pacific Ocean, forming the Columbia River bar. It pours into the ocean at twice the volume of water carried by the Mississippi River to the Atlantic Ocean. Sand and silt from the river's approximate two hundred fifty nine thousand square-mile drainage area pile up at the mouth of the river, forming the bar. The river is going out and the ocean waves are coming in, making tremendous waves. Sand bars and unpredictable currents motivate mariners to approach it with caution and respect.

Ken told me he would supply the boat and gas. I was to bring the food and drink. That was easy. I would bring water, soda, sandwiches and chocolate chip cookies.

He picked us up on Friday evening after work. Even though it was summer, I knew that it would be cold during the early morning and evening. Warm clothes would be necessary. Ken was experienced and knew how to maneuver the boat going over the bar. I thought that it would be fun to go fishing with the boys again. The ocean was smooth and the fishing was great once you got across the bar!

I gave Yvonne a call and told her the name and phone number of the hotel we were staying at. I told her the name of the boat, *The Cruiser*. She reminded me to be careful and bring home lots of fish.

We drove to the ocean Friday night, got the boat in the water and had everything set up for early Saturday morning. We were all up very early and had a good breakfast. We filled our thermos jug with hot coffee. What a perfect day to go fishing! The weather couldn't be better. We got to the boat a little before daylight. We arrived at the dock, checked out our gear, and we were on our way.

We were straightening out our lines and putting on the bait as we headed toward the bar. The bait we used was frozen herring. I noticed the boat was sitting a little low in the back where Ken had set the gas cans. I asked him why he had brought so much gas with him and he said he wanted plenty of gas so we wouldn't run out. Ken wasn't worried about it, so we let it alone. It was cold and windy out on the ocean, so we all stayed close to the cab. Ken checked out his radio and it was working. We poured ourselves each a cup of the hot coffee. The warm cups kept our hands warm.

This sure was a lot different from going out with my company. On the bigger boats, the cabin is closed in and, as a result, we didn't notice the cold. We were approaching the bar and observed that the waves were huge. The waves crashed against the front of the boat and the mist seemed as though it engulfed us. Ken maneuvered the boat, heading straight into the waves. By the time we got through the first wave, the force of the water had turned the boat sideways.

We could see the second wave coming and we were in trouble. Ken tried to maneuver the boat and be ready for the next wave but it was too late. The wave engulfed us and the boat was full of water and going down. Ken quickly grabbed the radio and called SOS. I looked around frantically and saw a big white boat coming alongside us and two men in white clothes. They tossed me a rope and told me to hold it. They told the boys to jump into their boat when they were right alongside. Joe, Chris and Ken jumped to the other boat. As soon as they were safely in the other boat, I jumped in.

It wasn't long before all we could see of Ken's boat was the round hook on the bow of the boat. The rest was under water. The front of the boat had an air pocket that kept the boat from sinking. The captain of the white boat called the Coast Guard and gave them our position. The captain said they would stay with us until the Coast Guard got there.

Amidst all the excitement I didn't get the name of the white boat or the captain's name, or how they happened to be right beside us. I think they were angels the Lord had sent to save us. At the time I didn't even think about it.

All I could think of was our boat was sinking and we were safe on another boat. I said a quick, "Thank you, Lord."

We stayed there until the Coast Guard arrived. They asked us if we needed any medical help. We let them know that we were fine and very pleased to be safe. A diver in a wet suit swam to Ken's boat and attached a clip to it. They started the winch and pulled Ken's boat halfway up out of the water. The Coast Guard called the captain of the white boat and asked him if we wanted him to transfer us to the Coast Guard boat. He said no, that it would be easier for him to just take us into the dock. We thanked him and offered to pay him for our rescue. He wouldn't accept any money. He said, "Some day I may need help" and left.

My son, Steven, was driving to the coast to meet us and spend some time fishing with us. On the way to the coast he was listening to the radio. A news flash came over the radio quite a few times saying a boat named *The Cruiser* had sunk. Steve knew that we were on *The Cruiser*. They didn't say whether or not there had been any survivors. Steve was very concerned.

We were already back at the hotel by the time Steven arrived. He was very happy to see us. He told us the news he had heard on the radio. He urged me to call Mom and let her know what had happened before she heard it on the radio. She had not heard it yet and told me, "The Lord is looking out for you." She was thankful that the boys and I were out of danger and Steven got there safely. We returned home safe and secure later in the day.

We spent the night reminiscing to take our minds off our present situation. God was teaching us something through this ordeal. We knew that God doesn't allow anything to happen in our lives without a purpose. Even the unintentional things we do. He will turn them around and help us to learn. It was obvious that if we returned safely, it would be a miracle. We were at the end of our rope.

God had provided us with our campsite. We were so well protected down deep in the woods that we didn't know that the worst blizzard in many years was blowing just up the mountain. From our vantage point, when we looked up, we could feel the snowflakes on our faces.

After what seemed like an eternity, we could see a faint light peeking through the tall pine trees. We put all the wood we had on the fire. We stopped gathering wood and stood as close as possible to the fire. Everything but our boots was pretty dry.

CHAPTER FIVE

FOLLOWING THE RIVER

*Hear my cry, O God; Give heed to
my prayer.*

Psalm 61:1

B oys, time to get your rifles and gear and get ready to move out," I said. I noticed Joe looking around in the snow in front of the fire. I asked him what he was looking for.

He told me, "I dropped a shell in front of the fire last night. I'm trying to find it."

I reminded him that the bed of coals was about three times as large as it was last night and the shell was probably under the coals this morning. We all three thanked the Lord that it didn't explode in the middle of the night. I told Joe, "Forget it, let's go home!"

As we left camp, we discovered that our tracks had been covered by newly fallen snow. I honestly thought that we would be able to follow our tracks back to our own trail and be back at the truck pretty fast. I didn't know about the fierce snowstorm. All of our tracks had long since been covered by the newly fallen snow. When we realized that we couldn't follow our tracks, we should have returned to our camp and waited to be rescued.

We reasoned that we had about twelve hours of daylight in which to find a road out. Surely we could find a road by then. The boys and I talked it over, and although Chris felt that we should try to retrace our footprints by memory, Joe and I agreed that to continue on down the hill would lead us to a road.

Chris, being outnumbered, was obliged to do it our way. We trudged on down the hill. What we didn't know was that we were a long way below all of the roads that lead out of the Hell Hole! Hunters had been lost in the Hell Hole in the past and sometimes they didn't get out alive. It was a very deep valley with cliffs on each side.

In the meantime, our hunting partner had walked back to the truck and waited for us. When we didn't return after quite a wait, he started to walk out to the guard shack. Before he got very far, he saw a jeep full of hunters. He related his story to them. As soon as they heard what happened they made a quick u-turn and sped down the mountain to the guard shack. They called the sheriff and told him what had happened. He said that he would organize a search party as soon as possible.

The hunters were eager to help in any way they could, so back up the mountain they went. They found room for Chuck, so he went along with them. For several hours, they drove up and down the roads yelling and honking their horn. They stopped from time to time and shined their lights down into the woods. Other hunters, hearing what had happened, covered other roads honking their horns. We were too far down in the hell hole to hear any of them or to see the lights.

After about an hour of wandering and not knowing

where we were heading, I was sure that we had lost all sense of direction. Finally we came to the crest of a hill and below us we saw a creek. Since water runs downhill, I was certain that if we could get to the creek and follow it, we would find our way out.

We walked, slid, fell, and climbed down the hill. I think that it was as steep a hill as I have ever been down. As we climbed down, we jumped from log to snow bank and from snow bank to log. Sometimes we fell through and had to pull ourselves back up on top of the log. A few times we jumped and hit right on solid logs. We all thanked the Lord for protecting us from broken bones on that excursion down the mountain.

When we finally reached the bottom of the mountain, the terrain flattened out and was a lot easier walking. What a relief to make it down that mountain! We reached the bottom of the mountain about ten o'clock in the morning. We were elated! We thought we were on our way out at last. Little did we know what lay ahead of us.

We hadn't walked more than a couple hundred yards when I saw something through the trees. Initially I thought that it was a house but I didn't say anything because I didn't want to get the boys' hopes up, only to be mistaken. As I got closer, I saw that it wasn't a house. It was the worst thing it could ever be. Turned out it was a cliff that was straight up and down. Our hopes were dashed again.

The creek we were following went through a very narrow space in the cliff. There wasn't enough room for a person to get through. There was not enough space for us to follow the creek any farther. I knew that we must not get wet. We all three looked up at that cliff. There was one thing to do, and that was go up and over the cliff. It was about seventy- five or eighty feet straight up. We were not relishing the idea of climbing again.

We backtracked about a hundred yards or so and then angled towards the cliff as we began our ascent. There were a lot of downed trees that we had to scale and it was tough going. By the time we reached the top, Chris had developed leg cramps so bad that he was continually falling down. He wasn't a complainer, and we knew that his legs were hurting badly.

At that point we decided that we better stop for a rest and then continue down the other side of the cliff. After another treacherous climb, we made it to the creek again. At this time we rested and had our last morsel of food. We each had a box of raisins, a real feast. We ate slowly and enjoyed every raisin. Soon it was time to push on.

It wasn't long before we came to another cliff. This time it was a little different; there was a log across the creek. We could bypass the cliff by crossing over the creek. We walked about another hundred yards and there was our third cliff. There was a log we could cross back over to our original side of the creek.

Joe and I made it across just fine, but Chris had trouble trying to walk on the log. It was tough for him to keep his balance. On the way over he slipped and got one of his legs soaking wet in the icy, cold water.

When he lost his balance, he also lost his gloves. Joe and I shared our gloves with Chris, swapping back and forth so that our hands wouldn't freeze.

We started following the creek again. We hadn't gone far when we found ourselves facing yet another cliff. I began to wonder if this would end. I didn't think there were this many cliffs in the entire state. But there it was and this time there were no logs to get across on. There were some large rocks spaced far apart. I wasn't sure we could make it across. Were the rocks too far apart? We all three decided to give it a try. We tossed our rifles over and watched as one of Joe's gloves slid off his hand and floated down the creek. Now we had three gloves for six hands.

By this time I was beginning to get worried about Chris. He already was very cold and had trouble crossing the creek. By the time he got across the creek, both of his feet were soaked. Now he was wet and cold. He was beginning to tire out rapidly and was unable to carry his rifle any longer. I considered leaving it, but it belonged to Steven. I slung it over my shoulder and carried two.

Chris was cold and extremely exhausted by this time. He was getting worse with every step. He was pretty tough so I knew that when he said he was cold, he meant it. Joe and I were cold too, and all three of us were getting cramps in our legs. No matter what we did, we all knew we had to keep pushing on. We walked down the creek a little farther and wouldn't you know it, another cliff. Chris said that he couldn't make it any farther. He just wanted to sit down, rest and sleep. I knew if we fell asleep we would never wake up.

Looking up this new hill, we thought we saw a flat place that might be a road. I told the boys we would rest as soon as we got to the flat place. This gave the boys fresh energy to keep going. When we got to the old logging road, we saw what appeared to be footprints. There was enough snow in them so we couldn't tell if they were human or animal prints. I told the boys that they sure looked like human prints to me. We followed the old logging road around a few bends only to be disappointed again. It led to an abrupt slope down to the creek. Again the prints and the old logging road led to nowhere.

In the distance we could see a clearing in the trees

and felt sure that this was an end to the hills. It was either up or down, and up seemed best. Chris was extremely exhausted by now and said he just couldn't climb another step. Joe and I told him to climb and we would help him as much as possible. Joe led the way and I got behind Chris and pushed. Joe and I both encouraged Chris and helped him make each step.

CHAPTER SIX

MEANWHILE, BACK HOME

I will sing to the Lord, because He has dealt bountifully with me.

Psalm 13:6

I was cold and my feet were wet as I climbed up another steep hill. I began thinking about home and the pleasant Thanksgiving Day we had together. Don and Steve couldn't come home. They were both studying for finals. I sure missed them when they weren't home for a holiday.

Thanksgiving Day was relaxing for me. Yvonne was up early stuffing the turkey and preparing the food for dinner. The delicious fragrance of turkey roasting began to fill the house. It made me hungry. Soon the children were setting the table with our very best silverware and dishes.

The only guest we had invited was Grandpa Carl. He was a special guest at our house on most occasions. He lived a few miles from us, and our children had adopted him as their grandpa. He seemed to enjoy spending time with us and thrived in the commotion of a big family for a few hours.

Even though he lived alone, he was very social. He would recite the Lord's Prayer for us in German. My children loved to sit on his lap and at his feet and listen to him tell them about the way life used to be. He was knowledgeable about the world around him and was quite astute politically. He was a vegetarian most of his life. He went to church with us and seemed pleased to be a part of our family. He liked the music at our church and tapped his feet to the beat. By the time I took him home in the evening, he was exhausted and ready to go to his nice, quiet home.

My children loved to wrestle with me. They would all pile on me and try to hold me down. They never were able to do so, but they never gave up trying.

Later in the day, Chris and I played a game of checkers. It lasted a long time. We spent a lot of time thinking and planning our moves.

Then it was Friday morning, the day after Thanksgiving. Our house was busy as usual. Joe got up early and started the fire in our fireplace. He enjoyed having it all cozy and warm when the rest of us got up. Since we all had the day off, none of us were in any hurry to get up.

I especially liked holidays with Yvonne and the kids. If it snowed out, all the kids and I would build forts and have big snowball fights. Once in awhile I could get Yvonne to come out and join in all the fun. The little ones and I were always on one team, and all of the older kids were on the other team. Let me tell you, we had some snowball fights! They would go on for hours. There were a lot of trees to hide behind. Each team would try to sneak up on the other. The team that had the best advantage would pepper the other team with snowballs. We would all be covered with snow!

This year my extended family all got together in Colorado Springs, Colorado, for a big Thanksgiving dinner on the Saturday after Thanksgiving. My older brother, Tom, had the dinner at his house. We didn't attend this year. The weather was unpredictable and I wanted a quiet weekend with my own family. Little did I know. The weekend was anything but quiet!

Then I was on the phone with my hunting partner, Chuck. I hung up and said, "The boys and I are going hunting for a few hours with Chuck. It will give me a chance to see what my new four-wheeler will do out in the snow."

My daughter told me later that the house got much quieter after the boys and I left. That was hard for me to believe! They sewed, read books and watched television. It started snowing quite hard during the early afternoon and continued on into the night. Through the big front windows, the kids could see the big, soft snowflakes falling ever so quietly. It was a peaceful winter scene.

Mom prepared dinner for the family. It was starting to get dark, so she fed the younger children and put dinner in the oven to keep it warm for us mighty hunters. A little after dark, Yvonne got a phone call from Chuck. He was at the guard shack and he told her that the two boys and I had not returned to the truck. He told her it was snowing quite hard there.

Chuck told my wife that he had called the sheriff and he was organizing a search party as soon as possible. He assured her that other hunters were out there driving up and down the roads, honking their horns and calling out as loud as they could for me and the boys. He told her not to worry, we would soon be home.

She told me later that she felt pretty sure that we would soon be out on the road with our elk. Carrying an elk out is no small undertaking. It takes a lot of time and energy. We had hunted all over the state and had never even come close to getting lost.

It was getting quite late by this time. The guard shack called her again and said they were concerned because the weather was bad. The guard told her that it was the worst snowstorm they had seen in a long time. They assured her that they were doing all they could. They planned to have a search team go in as soon as possible in the morning. She said that she could hear the urgency in his voice.

Chuck got on the phone and told Yvonne that he was so very sorry. My wife and I had been friends with Chuck and his wife for a long time. When Chuck got that serious, she knew things were not going well.

My wife immediately called her brother, Arlo, and told him what was happening. He was an experienced hunter and had recently hunted in the area where we started our hunt. He drove out to the guard shack right away and stayed there all through the night and the next day until we all three were rescued. He didn't get any sleep until the rescue was completed.

She then called our neighbor and without delay he called other neighbor men. They all hopped in his four-wheeler and drove to the guard shack. They were given permission to drive up and down the mountainous roads honking their horn and flashing a light down into the thick woods. They kept Yvonne updated on what they were doing.

I heard from Yvonne later that a lot was happening at home while we were lost in the wilderness. Without delay my wife called our pastor and told him the situation. He prayed with her and called the elders in the church. The prayer chain was activated. Our church, Scholl's Community Church, and Pastor James Moore, believed that we serve a God who answers prayer. The people at the church loved the Lord and knew how to pray.

She called my supervisor at the plant, and he in turn called my co-workers. My wife told me later that she received many, many calls offering help. When they asked how they could help, she told everyone who called to pray. Yvonne and I had been foster and adoptive parents for a few years and she said some of the women who called expressed concern for the children and how they were going to take this.

Many kind Christian friends and neighbors asked Yvonne if they could come to our house that night and be with her and the children. She told them that the younger children needed to get a good night's sleep and she preferred to talk with them in the morning, before anyone got there. Mom wanted to let them know what was happening and to have prayer with them. She felt they needed to have time to talk about what was happening, as well.

I learned how kind Christian friends are. You just don't know what their friendship means to you until a crisis and they are right there to help. I hope that I am that thoughtful and kind to other people when they are in need.

The guard shack kept contact with Yvonne all night. They were very kind to her, but they didn't give any hope that the boys and I would be found alive. When my wife wasn't on the phone, she was on her knees praying. Chuck told her that the sheriff's posse was organizing a search and rescue team. At the crack of dawn they would begin searching the area. I was told later that there were about five hundred men at the guard shack ready to go in and begin searching as soon as the gate was opened.

The men of one family from our church were experienced hunters and were familiar with the logging roads in the region. They tirelessly spent hours searching for us. Their sister, Lita, later married my son, Steven. I always appreciated their concern for us and willingness to make sacrifices in their effort to help us.

Yvonne was comforted knowing that the boys and I knew Jesus as Lord and Savior. The Lord was near and dear to her that night. He gave her loving words from the book of Psalms. She said that she wept at times. It must have been a difficult night.

More friends and neighbors called and said they were heading out to the guard shack and would drive up and down the mountain on every road honking their horns. They would shine their lights down into the woods. They updated her every so often to let her know if there was a response. Mom made known to everyone who called that Bill and the boys believed in Jesus Christ as their Savior and they were ready to go be with Him if that was what happened.

Yvonne told me later that she felt that she should wait until the next morning to tell the younger ones. She made sure all the children were snuggled under their warm quilts in their beds and sound asleep.

Before saying their prayers with them, she let them know that daddy and the boys were delayed and they weren't quite sure why. She did not want them to know how severe the situation was. Each one of the children prayed that God would take care of daddy and the boys.

Mom told me later that all the kids were up bright and early the next morning. They were looking forward to going outside to play in the snow. They had all kinds of plans. She gathered them all around her and told them that Daddy and the boys had not come home yet. She assured them there were many people trying to help them.

By nine in the morning our house was full of caring people from our church. They brought food and games. One lady brought activities to keep the children occupied, so that Yvonne could be on the phone with all the people who were calling her with updates about the situation.

A friend of ours was prepared to call our sons in college and let them know what was happening, if we received bad news. Yvonne gave him their phone numbers and he would call them. She planned to call them too. She was concerned that so many people would be calling and coming to the house that she might be overwhelmed. The guard shack called Yvonne often during the day to keep her updated on what was happening. My brother-in-law, Arlo, kept her informed of any new information, as well.

CHAPTER SEVEN

THE SWEET SOUND OF HELICOPTERS

In Your presence is fullness of joy.

Psalm 16:11

We followed the logging roads time and again, only to be disappointed each time. Joe led the way and I pushed Chris to help him keep going. Chris was very tired by now and said that he couldn't climb another step. Joe and I encouraged him to keep on climbing and we would help him as much as possible.

Chris stopped suddenly and said, "Listen, I hear something. What's that noise?"

We all stopped but we heard no sounds. There was complete silence.

Then we heard what sounded like a flapping noise, then a whirring sound. I yelled, "It's a helicopter!

We raced back to the clearing as fast as we could run and tried to see where the whirring sound was coming from. I grabbed the rifle from my shoulder and quickly slammed a shell in the chamber.

We kept our eyes peeled toward the sky but we didn't see or hear anything. After what seemed like an eternity a helicopter came into sight. It was the prettiest sight we had ever seen, and oh the sound of those blades! Finally there it was in line right over us. When it got to the right spot, I fired off a shot. The helicopter went about a quarter of a mile, made a stop, turned, and headed straight toward us.

We jumped up and down and hollered as loud as we could. Amidst all the excitement, Chris yelled over and over again, "They saw us, they saw us!"

The helicopter came right up to our ridge and stopped just over us. It was so close we could see the pilot and co-pilot. We could see two search and rescue people in the back. We were sure they saw us. You never saw three happier hunters!

To our dismay, they turned and went right back up the valley and out of sight. We three looked at each other and said, "This can't be happening." Needless to say, we were all pretty discouraged. I told the boys that we better get busy and get a fire started so they would see our smoke if they come back around. It would keep us warm, as well. I knew that Chris would not last another night in the bitter cold. My hope was almost gone. I thought to myself that they would not return to this ridge, having just searched this area and apparently seeing no one. We had to do something.

We all decided that our only hope at this time was to look to God, who was our strength and our only hope. We stood together and prayed. We each prayed that we would be able to get a fire going and the helicopters would return to the ridge we were standing on. We knew that we served a God of the impossible.

We began breaking up branches to build the fire but

we were on a steep slope, making it difficult to get to the trees and break off the branches. It was so steep that we had to hang onto a good branch with one hand and use the other hand to break off the dry branches. Somehow with great difficulty we managed to forage enough dry branches for a small fire.

I took our second bag of pitch and placed it under the branches we had gathered. Where would we find the dry paper to get the fire going? The only paper we had left was in our wallets. We gleaned some dry paper from our wallets. I had a twenty-dollar bill and two ones. It was difficult parting with those bills, but I knew that I had to. Chris and Joe had eight one-dollar bills between them. None of us were complaining one bit. We were glad that we had the bills. We agreed they might save our lives. Money doesn't have quite the same value when you are dealing with life and death issues.

I ever so carefully put the dry bills under the pitch and lit the fire. We were all three standing over the fire praying for God to intervene! Just a small spark and then it started burning slowly. Soon we knew we had it going, and it looked like we could leave it and gather more wood.

Joe and I insisted that Chris stay close by the fire and make sure it kept going. He was wet and freezing cold. He looked so young and vulnerable standing there with his hands over the small fire. We wanted him as close to the fire as possible, hoping his clothes would dry out and his hands would warm up a little. His hands were very cold and he was rapidly losing hope.

Joe and I left the fire to go and look for more wood. About that time, Chris looked up and saw the helicopter searching another ridge about two miles straight out in front of us! He yelled to Joe and I to come quickly. "Come quick, quick. I think the helicopter is coming back!"

I ran back to our makeshift camp and grabbed my rifle. I fired off one of our two remaining shells.

Unknown to us, my hunting partner Chuck, and my brother-in-law Arlo, were back at the guard shack where we initially began our hunt. They heard our first two shots even though the helicopter had not heard them. Both of them were quite familiar with the area, so they knew exactly where our first shots came from. This assured them we were still alive.

They in turn relayed this information to the ground control search and rescue team. They contacted the helicopter radioman. They were attempting to zero in on our location.

I didn't know what was happening or what, if any, information was being transmitted. I was standing there in the snow with my rifle in my hands, watching as the helicopter turned around and went back behind the ridge. Unbeknown to us the helicopter was still searching the area where we first got lost. At noon they found our first campsite. They put down the first ground search and rescue team to search for us on foot. After it was all over, I knew that the boys were right and we should have stayed at our first campsite.

This would have saved our strength. We could have kept the fire going and we would have been warm. We could have taken turns sleeping. The search and rescue team would have found us much sooner.

It was about two and a half hours since we had seen or heard the helicopter. There wasn't much daylight left. I told the boys that there was a good chance the helicopters wouldn't find us until tomorrow. We were all three wet and tired.

I learned later that my sister-in-law had organized a rescue center and was transmitting information from one rescue unit to another and from ground to helicopter. At this time the rescue unit had decided that they were low on gas and had to go back to their unit and fill their tanks. When their gas tanks were filled, they felt that it was too late and there wasn't enough daylight left for them to go back and search the mountain. They planned to stay at the base and resume the search early the next morning.

My sister-in-law began making calls to find out why

they had called off the search for the day. Every number she called transferred her to another number. Finally she was transferred to the basement and the janitor answered the phone.

She was not one to be deterred. Immediately she called the Office of the Governor of Oregon and told them there were three hunters lost in the mountains and two of them were teenagers. She told them they had heard gun shots and felt certain that the hunters were still alive. She advised them that there was enough daylight hours for them to continue the rescue effort. She insisted they fly over the area where they heard the gunshots.

She felt there was enough daylight left to rescue them without harm to the rescuers or the hunters. Apparently the Governor's office agreed. The helicopters with the rescue team on board were on their way to the mountain. I am very grateful for an excellent team and their willingness to put forth so much effort to find us.

We were all very cold. I let the boys know that we better find a campground and start looking for firewood. I turned and looked up the mountain. It was the steepest terrain that we had encountered so far. I realized that Chris could go no farther. He was so exhausted and cold that his whole body was shivering. I gave him the job of staying by the campfire and he was to keep it going. We wanted him to get warm. Joe and I told him that we would go up the mountain and try to find a flat place to make fire and prepare for another cold night in the Oregon wilderness. We encouraged Chris to be strong and keep the fire going. "We'll all be alright, Chris. We'll be right back for you."

Joe and I reluctantly started up the mountain. It was so steep we had to move on our hands and knees and use our rifles as levers. It was tough going with some snowdrifts up to our waists. At times we would get cramps in our legs and oh did they hurt! It seemed to me that we were never going to find a flat spot.

About halfway up we saw some big logs that might work for a campsite. As quickly as I could, I climbed over the logs and began to clear a spot in the snow to try and build a fire. Joe went out to look for wood. The more I dug, the deeper the snow got. I finally realized that this was no place to build a fire, the snow would keep putting it out. I learned that lesson the hard way at our first campsite. Joe returned with no wood. We decided to go on up the mountain. Finally we found a big fir tree with a flat spot underneath it. I started breaking up branches and Joe went out looking for bigger wood. While looking for wood, Joe found a clearing at the top of the mountain.

Meanwhile I leaned both rifles against a big fir tree and began to assess my fire building supplies. They were pretty meager. I pulled out my last pack of pitch and the last dry paper out of my pocket. My last dry paper consisted of my hunting license and elk tag. I started the fire with my last pack of pitch and my license and tag. That was enough to get the fire going and I was one happy hunter.

Whirrrrr! whirrrrr! Whirrrrr! What was that? The helicopter was returning! I could hear it coming down the valley toward us! Chris heard it too. He jacked the last shell into the chamber, but the breech was blocked with ice. He reached out to take the shell out of the action and put it safely in his jacket. His hands were so cold and stiff that they were numb. As he tried to take the shell out, he dropped in on the ground and couldn't find it in the deep snow. He started waving wildly and yelling as loud as he could. He was moving around and jumping up and down.

The helicopter made several passes down the valley, looking straight down trying to locate us. The search and rescue team spotted Chris frantically waving. The helicopter turned and came in as close as possible to pick up Chris. As they hovered over him, they sent down a medic and a winch. The medic strapped Chris in the hoist and they brought him up to the helicopter. They sent down the hoist again and picked up the medic.

Chris was very cold but safe and on his way to the nearest hospital. They asked Chris if there were any other survivors and he said no! He was cold and pretty well out of it. A little later he told them that Joe and I were on up the mountain.

I could see them picking up Chris. I was so grateful to see Chris rescued. I breathed a big sigh of relief. The mountain was so steep that I looked down on the prop. I could hear Joe yelling and waving. I grabbed both rifles and ran as fast as I could. I didn't know that I could run so fast! Joe had taken off his coat and was waving it over his head and he was yelling as loud as he could. He looked like a crazy, wild man!

The helicopter came up, flew over us and passed us right by. In moments they were out of sight. Soon they returned and came right to us. They told us over a bullhorn that they saw us and would return. The winch was broken and they had to return to base and get another. "Stay where you're at, we'll be back for you!"

Joe and I settled down to wait for them. We were feeling relaxed and hopeful that we would not have to spend another night in the wilderness. The sun peeked through the clouds for a few minutes and we soaked it all in, loving every minute of it.

The helicopter was back in about half an hour. They dropped down a medic first. He got out of the hoist and ran over to us. "Are you OK? Do you have any broken bones?" He checked for frostbite and found that we showed no signs of it. He said that they didn't expect to find anyone alive. The storm was severe and it was bitter cold. "I'm glad to see someone who knows what they are doing in the woods."

I told him that if we knew what we were doing, we wouldn't be lost!

He encouraged us when he told us that hunters lost that long in such severe weather rarely make it out alive. He warned us to get in the hoist fast, due to the chill factor caused by the props. With the chill factor, it was thirty degrees below zero. Joe and I quickly climbed into the hoist and the medic strapped us in. We found out what he meant by the cold air from the blades! They began pulling us up slowly. We were about two feet up and we swung out over the hill, which put us at about six feet up in the air. At that height, the hoist broke and Joe and I fell. We landed on the top of a small tree. Joe and I looked at each other and wondered what was going on. We both agreed that they must know what they were doing, but this sure was a funny way to get us up to the helicopter.

At this time the medic told us to get out of the hoist fast. The pilot had radioed him and told him that the winch had broken. They had to go get another helicopter. I don't know what the medic was thinking. He had just come down with the help of that winch. They threw a survival pack down to us.

The pilot told the medic that there was a road about three fourths of a mile on up the mountain. He told him the directions to get to it and left. The medic gave us dry clothes. We looked in the pack and found only one change of dry clothes. I told Joe to change into the dry clothes. I knew that he was cold and I could wait.

The medic offered us warm food, but we declined. We wanted to find the road and then we would feel like eating. He gave us some beef jerky and we headed for the road. As we began climbing the mountain, each step seemed like the last step that I could take. I didn't have any more energy. I thought that I couldn't take one more step, but somehow we kept on walking, one step at a time.

About five minutes before we found the road, the helicopter came back. They had landed and sent Chris by ambulance to the hospital. They felt he had frostbite on his hands and feet and needed to be treated at the hospital. Then they returned for us.

The copter stayed right overhead and directed the medic to the road where they wanted to pick us up. We turned right and walked a couple of hundred yards up the road where it intersected with another road. These were old logging roads with some overgrowth. They felt this would be the safest place to pick us up.

They let down the hoist and Joe and I got on as quickly as we could. Everything was going just fine as they lifted us up. We got to the bottom of the helicopter and the hoist stopped very suddenly. I could just reach the railing. The search and rescue man tried to get the hoist to move us up but it wouldn't budge. I said, "Lord, You've brought us this far, don't let us fall." I looked down and it was a long way to the ground! I didn't want to fall onto another tree from this height! The medic working the winch told us to let go of the rails. "I have to let you back down a few feet."

The hoist fell about ten feet and stopped suddenly. Joe and I looked at each other and we both agreed, "What's the difference if we freeze to death or we fall and die?" We both smiled and right about then the hoist began moving upward again. It jerked a little and then went up fairly smoothly. We got into the helicopter safely and we were ready to go home!

They picked up the medic and away we went. Joe and I were singing "Homeward Bound!"

The hospital called Yvonne and told her Chris was fine and she could pick him up. The roads were still icy and slippery, so our pastor drove Yvonne to the hospital to pick up Chris. The emergency room doctor informed her that Chris did not have any signs of frostbite. They told her he was just fine and could go home with her. Chris was smiling and looking forward to going home.

Within a few hours we were all safe and snug in our home with an experience that none of us would ever forget.

No! We didn't get our elk!

CHAPTER EIGHT

AFTER WORDS

It is good to give thanks to the Lord.

Psalm 92:1

Thank you for reading the story of one of the greatest adventures of my life. This adventure nearly turned into tragedy for my two sons and me. I give all the credit to the Lord. He protected us through the raging blizzard and the cold, dark night. I learned some things about my own personal pride and my responsibility to others.

The Lord kept us from freezing to death when all the odds were against us. If we had not been rescued when we were, my family would have been changed forever. Chris, Joe and I would have missed out on so much.

I have every reason to be one happy guy. I found out that I have relatives, friends and neighbors who didn't hesitate to step out and put themselves at risk in order to offer us help. The unbelievable part was that even complete strangers assisted in the search. They heard that two boys and their dad were lost in the worst blizzard that had come through the mountains in many years. Many of these men put themselves in harm's way to assist in making sure that the boys and I walked out of there alive. I thank the Lord for these people. I'm not sure they realize all they did for Chris, Joe and me that day.

The rescue team and the helicopter pilot were instrumental in rescuing us. Their expertise and dedication were outstanding. The helicopter pilot was experienced at flying in unusually bad weather. In the worst of circumstances, he was able to maneuver the helicopter in the unbelievably treacherous mountain terrain. The cliffs were steep and the trees were tall. At times during the rescue the pilot hovered dangerously at treetop level.

Arlo, and his wife, kept all the search efforts coordinated. Arlo proficiently organized search efforts from the shack at the guard gate. His wife effectively arranged all the parts of the search from her home, including the helicopter search and rescue team. She kept very busy tracking the entire rescue endeavor. She maintained close contact with everyone involved in the search.

She called one of the organizations that was taking an active part in the rescue operation. They kept transferring her telephone call until finally she was transferred to the janitor in the basement of the building. He said that he was just mopping the floor and didn't know anything about any lost hunters or a search and rescue team.

She became very concerned since time was a major factor. It was winter and there was only a limited amount of daylight. At that crucial point she called the Governor's office regarding keeping the search and rescue team active in the search during the afternoon. They had been ordered to return to base and begin the search again the next morning, weather allowing.

She advised the Governor that their was a break in the weather with at least three to four hours of daylight left and the search must continue. She did not feel that the boys and I would live through another night in the frigid temperatures. I believe that my boys and I lived through this ordeal thanks to her quick and capable action on our behalf. I could never thank her enough for all she did for us.

I love to spend time out in the wide open spaces fishing and hunting. The sport is great, but I think the best part of it is sitting around the warm fire at night watching the sparks fly and light up the woods around us each time more wood is thrown on the fire. My boys asked me if the stories told around the campfire are really true. "You will have to decide that for yourself," I answered, with a big smile on my face. Along with all the storytelling, there's all that good food cooked over the open campfire! Most of the daylight hours are spent walking. At nightfall sleep comes easy in the fresh, clear mountain air.

I always thought I was pretty tough and strong, but I learned real quick that no matter how tough I think I am, there comes a time when I have to trust in the strength of the Lord. During this adventure I came to the end of my own resources and knew that it would take a miracle of God to get us out alive. I knew all too well that I was responsible for two young boys.

I relied on some important words from the Bible that I learned long ago in Vacation Bible School. I encourage you to memorize them and keep them in your heart for that day when you are desperate and have reached the end of your own resources. Better yet, store them in your memory bank and be reminded of them every day.

The Shepherd Psalm

The Lord is my shepherd,
I shall not want.
He makes me lie down in green pastures:
He leads me beside quiet waters.
He restores my soul;
He guides me in the paths of righteousness
For His name's sake.
Even though I walk through the valley of the shadow
of death,
I fear no evil for You are with me;
Your rod and Your staff, they comfort me.
You prepare a table before me in the presence of my
enemies.
You have anointed my head with oil,
My cup overflows.
Surely goodness and kindness will follow me all the
days of my life.
And I will dwell in the house of the Lord forever.

Psalm 23

These are words to live by. I can tell you that from experience. They gave me strength during my unbelievably harsh experience in the freezing temperatures of the snow-covered mountains of Oregon.

The Lord's Prayer

Our Father who is in heaven,
Hallowed be Thy name.
Thy kingdom come.
Thy will be done,
On earth as it is in heaven.
Give us this day our daily bread,
And forgive us our debts
as we also have forgiven our debtors
And do not lead us into temptation
but deliver us from evil
For Thine is the kingdom and the power
and the glory forever.
Amen

Mathew 6:9-13

Here's a few more verses from the Old Testament Book of Proverbs that help me keep my life together. It is important to read from the book of Proverbs every day. It teaches you how to respond to every situation in your life. I hope these verses help you in your time of need. Take them to heart and make them a part of your life.

Trust in the Lord with all your heart
And do not lean on your own understanding
In all your ways acknowledge Him,
And He will make your paths straight.
Proverbs 3:5,6

For he who finds Me finds life And obtains favor
from the Lord.
Proverbs 9:3

In the fear of the Lord there
Is strong confidence
And his children will have refuge.
Proverbs 15:26

Did I learn any lessons from this dramatic experience? You bet I did. I have a new appreciation for the love and mercy of God. I recognized that I had not appreciated the love of my wife and family as much as I should.

It has taken me a while to complete this book. I sat down soon after I was rescued and hand-wrote everything that happened. A friend typed it for me and it has been in my desk ever since. It is time now to share my story with you. I hope you enjoy reading this incredible adventure and that you learn life lessons more easily and quickly than I have. Thanks for sticking with me through this story.

Profile of William Bush

William is thankful that he and the boys came out of their ordeal without any damage done. He learned things about preparing for a hunting trip as well as things not to do. William moved his wife and family to Prescott, Arizona in 1980, where he and his wife still live. He bought a grocery store on Gurley Street right in downtown Prescott. Later he established a successful construction company and ran it until he had a heart attack in 1987. He recuperated from the heart attack and retired from the building profession at that time.

He lives on four beautiful acres in Williamson Valley and continues to enjoy the outdoors. Working in his shop is a favorite pastime. William attends Alliance Bible Church in Prescott regularly and has many friends there. He is involved in the men's group and the early morning prayer meetings.

William enjoys seeing his children and grandchildren as often as possible. He visits them and talks with them on the phone as often as possible. The grandchildren say he is "cool."

William was very actively involved in the upbringing of his children. He spent as much time with them as possible. He loves his children and brags about all of them every chance he gets.

His wife believes that the reason the children turned out so well and are such successful young people is because he is an outstanding dad.

Profile of Chris Clark

Chris spent his early years with the Bush family in Scholls, Oregon. He quickly became a part of the family and continues to be to this day. During the summers he and the other children built rafts and swam in the creek that flowed through the property.

He loved being in the outdoors. He didn't spend any more time in the house than was necessary, especially the kitchen. There were many activities outdoors that were far more interesting to him. He enjoyed working with motors and liked to drive anything that had wheels.

Chris liked having his brother, Joe, live at our house. Each time Joe left, it would be difficult for Chris. He missed Joe a lot, but soon he would be outside having fun with the rest of the kids. He did well in school and learned to play the guitar.

Chris married a lovely young lady, Lynette, and they have two sons. Their sons are both in the United States Air Force. Lynette is an airline hostess for Horizon Air. They continue to be a part of the Bush family. Chris and his wife attend their church regularly and are actively involved. They have served on mission trips to various parts of the world, including Africa.

They live in Washington and Chris works for Boeing Aircraft. When he isn't working, his favorite recreation is riding his snowmobile out in the wilderness. He has gone on several hunting trips to remote areas of Idaho and Alaska. He has hunted moose and caribou.

Chris is a young man to be proud of. He is a loving husband and father.

His sons are outstanding young men.

Profile of Joe Clark

Joe lived with the Bush family four years
altogether: two years during the school year and
year-round for two years. He and Chris were
especially pleased when they could be together. He
was honored as the most improved student in his
entire class the second semester he was at our house,
and the following semester he was on the honor roll.

Joe loved to cook and often would make the family
breakfast. He would cook up some unusual dishes,
but they were usually eaten! One morning he made
pancakes for the family. He put blueberries in the
batter and stirred the batter until it turned blue. None
of the other children would eat the blue pancakes.

Second to cooking, Joe liked working with
landscaping and plants. He attended the youth group
at church and had many friends. Joe was not afraid
to speak up at school about something that he
recognized was wrong.

Occasionally, Joe would have a doctor's appointment
and he enjoyed it very much when Granny Bush,
William's mother, would take him to the appointment.
He knew there would be no more school for him that
day! After the appointment they would go bowling
and out to lunch and he could buy whatever he wanted
to eat. Joe was always kind and polite to Granny and
she enjoyed spoiling him.

After graduating from high school, Joe joined the United States Army. He died while serving in the military. William is confident that Joe believed in Jesus as his Savior and is now safely in the presence of the Lord.

William says he was honored to have been a part of Joe's life. "He will be in my heart and my family, and I will not forget him."

He was a fine young man.

CHAPTER NINE

EVERY MAN'S GUIDE TO THE SCRIPTURES

How great are Your works, O Lord.

Psalm 92:5

At one time or another all of us walk through dark and dangerous valleys in our lives. I hope the following will guide and encourage you as you deal with life's toughest issues.

Fear of the Lord:

Psalms 111:10

"The fear of the Lord is the beginning of wisdom."

Psalms 2:11

"Worship the Lord with reverence and rejoice with trembling."

Psalms 19:9

"The fear of the Lord is clean, enduring forever; the judgments of the Lord are true: they are righteous altogether."

If you want to be wise, respect God and read His word. Respect for Him will lead you to obedience to Him. A healthy respect (fear) of the Lord is essential in your Christian walk. It is important to understand that you do not become wise by life experience and education alone. God is our source of wisdom and His word is our guide. Read Psalm 111 often.

Discouragement:

Proverbs 19:3

"The foolishness of man ruins his ways and his heart rages against the Lord."

2 Kings 6:16

"So he (Elisha) answered, do not fear for those who are with us are more than those who are with them."

1 Thessalonians 5:11

"Therefore encourage one another and build up one another..."

King David was discouraged at times but he would remember God's resources.

He would be strengthened and encouraged as he recalled God's great love for him. Read Psalm 119 and be encouraged. Often we become discouraged when we focus on ourselves rather than on others and the Lord and His goodness.

Discouragement might be the disenchantment of self-love. When we are discouraged we usually direct our thinking toward ourselves and our own situation.

Lay it all out before the Lord and allow Him to comfort and teach you. He will teach if you are willing to put Him first in your life. Putting Him first includes reading your Bible daily and praying every day.

Pride:

Proverbs 16:18

"Pride goes before destruction, and a haughty spirit before a fall."

Proverbs 14:3

In the mouth of the foolish is a rod for his back, but the lips of the wise will protect."

James 4:6, 7, 8

God is opposed to the proud, but gives grace to the humble. Submit therefore to God. Resist the devil and he will flee from you. Draw near to God and He will draw near to you ..."

It is acceptable to know your accomplishments are important and to feel good about them. It is also healthy to acknowledge your successes. It is important to give credit where credit is due.

Pride becomes a problem when you exaggerate your successes and don't acknowledge those around you who helped with your success. Rather than be self-centered, think of others. Recognize and encourage the achievements of others. Read the book of Proverbs and look for all the teaching about pride.

Anger:

Ephesians 4:26

"Be angry and do not sin; do not let the sun go down on your anger."

Proverbs 15:18

"A hot tempered man stirs up strife, but the slow to anger calms a dispute."

Proverbs 14:29

"He who is slow to anger has great understanding, But he who is quick tempered exalts folly."

The Bible does not forbid anger, but teaches us to control it. He does not want us to handle conflict with an out-of-control approach. If we harbor anger in our hearts and lives, we run the risk of becoming bitter.

Withdrawing is the easiest way to deal with anger. Often people who harbor anger in their hearts remove themselves from the situation that makes them angry. Sooner or later the anger will have to be addressed if you want to have a peaceful walk with God.

Anger impacts every part of your life. It leads to impatience, sinful thoughts, words, actions, and a lack of self-control. Often we jump to conclusions about a person or situation that makes us angry.

A healthy approach is admitting there is anger. Then explore the causes. Evaluate the situation with another person you trust. It is humbling for us to admit that we are angry. It is not easy to admit weakness or failure.

Confess your anger to God and you can be certain He will forgive you. If you confess your sin to a fellow Christian you will be supported and he will pray for you.

<u>Sexual Sin:</u>

Proverbs 6:32

The one who commits adultery with a woman is lacking sense, he who would destroy himself does it."

James 1:14, 15

"But each one is tempted when he is carried away and enticed by his own lust. Then when lust has conceived, it gives birth to sin, and when sin is accomplished, it brings forth death."

Proverbs 28:13

"He who conceals his transgressions will not prosper, but he who confesses and forsakes them will find compassion."

The sex act in marriage makes two become one. To break that oneness by having sex with someone else brings great pain to your spouse. Confession and repentance are necessary; then, you must abandon and renounce the sin. It is important to get away from everything that reminds you of it. God is compassionate and forgiving toward us. Focus on God and read His word daily.

Bitterness:

Hebrews 12:15

"See to it that no one comes short of the grace of God; that no root of bitterness springing up causes trouble, and by it many be defiled."

Mathew 5:23-24

"...if you are presenting your offering at the altar, and there remember that your brother has something against you, leave your offering there before the altar and go; first be reconciled to your brother, and then come and present your offering."

Ephesians 4:31

"Let all bitterness and wrath and anger and clamor and slander be put away from you, along with all malice."

Do you ever have a right to be bitter? Is bitterness ever justified? You do not have any control over what others do or say. You do have control over how you respond to what others do or say. Nursing a grudge hurts you worse than it hurts the person who deeply offended you. Bitterness can destroy your health, affect your marriage and your children, and cause you to age prematurely. There are consequences for refusing to release an offender from paying for a perceived offense. Offering forgiveness helps to mend the other person's pain as well as your own bitterness.

Forgiveness:

Ephesians 4:32

Be kind to one another, tender hearted, forgiving each other, just as God in Christ has forgiven you."

1 John 1:9

"If we confess our sins, He is faithful and righteous to forgive us our sins and cleanse us from all unrighteousness."

Colossians 1:13

"For He rescues us from the domain of darkness, and transfers us to the kingdom of His beloved son, in whom we have redemption, the forgiveness of sins."

Forgiveness opens the door to personal healing and tends to keep you from becoming angry or resentful. It is necessary to forgive often, just as Christ forgave you. There is no limit to forgiveness. It is a good idea to begin by forgiving ourselves. Sometimes it is easier to forgive others than to forgive ourselves for the things we've done. Once you've forgiven someone, stop dwelling on it and as soon as you can, start looking ahead.

ABOUT THE CO-AUTHOR
Yvonne Rose Bush

When asked, "What is the most rewarding thing you have done in your lifetime? The author's response is, "Raising my children." Yvonne Bush is the author of two books, the co-author of this book, and has completed the research for her fourth book, Living the Life, A Study in the Book of Philippians.

For the past ten years, Yvonne has been a Hearing Officer in Prescott Justice Court, Small Claims Division. She has served on the Board of Directors of Willow Creek Charter School, as well. Her biography is in Marquis "Who's Who of American Women," as well as other Marquis publications. One out of every five thousand women is profiled in Marquis "Who's Who of American Women."

She has traveled extensively, internationally on mission trips. She volunteered in the cancer unit of a large children's hospital in Moscow, Russia, in orphanages in Romania, and taught in junior/senior high schools in Romania. She spoke at a conference on child development in Taipei, Taiwan. She saw the vulnerability and the needs of children and as a result, sent much needed supplies to hospitals and orphanages.

Yvonne has an A.A. in General Education from Yavapai College, B.A. in Counseling/Psychology from Prescott College, an M.A. in Counseling/Psychology and Family Studies from Prescott College.

Also Written By Yvonne Rose Bush

Beyond Tears
A Book to Encourage Women

Bonding and Attachment

"Bonding and Attachment"
A Pamphlet

<u>NOTES</u>

<u>NOTES</u>

NOTES